Outsmarting
the Riptide of
Domestic Violence

Outsmarting the Riptide of Domestic Violence

Metaphor and Mindfulness for Change

Pat Pernicano, PsyD

JASON ARONSON
Lanham • Boulder • New York • Toronto • Plymouth, UK

Published by Jason Aronson
A wholly owned subsidiary of The Rowman & Littlefield Publishing Group, Inc.
4501 Forbes Boulevard, Suite 200, Lanham, Maryland 20706
www.rowmanlittlefield.com

Estover Road, Plymouth PL6 7PY, United Kingdom

British Library Cataloguing in Publication Information Available

Library of Congress Cataloging-in-Publication Data
Pernicano, Pat, 1954–
    Outsmarting the riptide of domestic violence : metaphor and mindfulness for
change / Pat Pernicano.
        p. cm.
    Includes bibliographical references and index.
    ISBN 978-0-7657-0885-4 (cloth : alk. paper) — ISBN 978-0-7657-0886-1
(electronic)
    1. Family violence—Psychological aspects. 2. Interpersonal relations—
Psychological aspects. 3. Self-actualization (Psychology) I. Title.
    HV6626.P457 2012
    362.82'92—dc23
                                                            2011044818

∞™ The paper used in this publication meets the minimum requirements of
American National Standard for Information Sciences—Permanence of Paper
for Printed Library Materials, ANSI/NISO Z39.48-1992.

Printed in the United States of America

Contents

Preface

I was discussing the use of metaphorical stories with my treatment team and telling them about my upcoming publication.

One of the therapists announced, "People *need* to buy your books, because your stories *work*. I can give you so many examples of times in women's group, family therapy, or child play therapy, where a story *opened things up* and got clients talking about more personal issues. We could finally do the therapy work they were *avoiding*!"

I replied, "I believe in the power of metaphor, but give me a few examples."

She offered, "This week, when my client said goodbye to her daughter, she didn't get all depressed like she usually would. She looked at me and said, '*It's like the story of the overstuffed nest. I'm launching my bird, and that's what she needs.*'"

Another therapist chimed in, "Yes, and you have to put that 'poop' story in the book."

I asked her why she particularly wanted that story.

She said, "After we read the story in family therapy, the metaphor really stuck with that mother. This week when one of the daughters was being mean to her brother, the mom looked at her and said, 'Stop it. You are flinging poop.' And the girl got a look in her eye and stopped."

Still another therapist added, "My client really had trouble separating the past from the present. She could not stop obsessing about things that went wrong before and expecting them to happen again. She said she was *Looking for Land Mines*. The Bottom Line at the end of the new story you wrote for her, *Looking for Land Mines in Disneyland,* has become her mantra: *Then Is Not Now.* It really helped her get through the treatment meeting with the DCS worker this week."

I hope this has whetted your appetite. I see it as my professional responsibility to share my stories with others. I know that you will find ways to use them with your own clients and thank you for that!

Acknowledgments

I am especially grateful to Julie Kirsch, my acquisitions editor for the first two volumes, for facilitating this new publication. She and I work well together, each of us dedicated to moving projects through to quick production. My husband Kevin has been gracious and understanding of the need for many occupied weekends and late nights so that I might complete this volume.

I would like to provide special thanks to Ashley Roberts, a Spalding University doctoral student, for her *read-through*, as she provided excellent feedback. Dr. Meg Hornsby, Alex Pruitt, Venice Anderson, Julie Housiaux, Lydia Watson, and Jessica Allen, my Spalding University doctoral therapy team, piloted the stories with their clients in family, group, and individual therapy and demonstrated their effectiveness with women and children. I am very appreciative of their open-mindedness, enthusiasm, and willingness.

But most importantly, I thank the clients I have worked with over the years; particularly those in the Family Preservation Program (FPP) at Providence House for Children, for these are their stories. Each woman arrived in our program at a different stage in the change process, and each story grew out of the issues faced in treatment. Their life experiences and the characters in these stories will be a source of light in the darkness of the lives of other women.

Introduction

Anyone that swims in the ocean knows about riptides, powerful currents that catch you in their grip and pull you out to sea. It's easy to drown in a riptide—when you fight or try to swim against the current it wears you down; and if you give up and go with the current you end up in deep water. You survive by using good strategy to outsmart the riptide. The secret of survival is to contra-intuitively move sideways until you are out of the current. Domestically violent relationships are a little like those powerful currents that threaten to pull you under or out to sea; and in such a relationship a woman's counteraggression or passivity can threaten her survival. A woman involved in domestic violence must go through a series of changes in order to escape the pull of a harmful relationship—she frees herself of the relational riptide by outsmarting her partner and moving in a new direction.

Current domestic violence intervention, often largely psycho-educational in nature, neglects some of the most crucial aspects of trauma-recovery; psycho-education is important, but it is like serving someone the icing without the cake. Trauma-Focused CBT (Cohen et al., 2006) provides a good framework for the services needed by those that witness and experience domestic violence; and the stories in this book may be used to implement each of the following PRACTICE elements: Psycho-education about domestic violence and trauma, Relaxation (and stress reduction), Affective Expression and regulation, Cognitive Restructuring, Trauma narrative development and processing, In vivo exposure to avoided situations, Conjoint sessions with children, and Enhancing future safety and healthy relationship/self-development.

Relational violence is complicated and crosses all social echelons. We are all susceptible to interpersonal misperception; and a woman can easily transform *Mr. Wrong* into *Mr. Right*, in spite of *evidence* to the contrary. "What did I see in him?" a woman asks, once the alcohol- or drug-enhanced attraction subsides, and her eyes and heart return to *normal*. "How could I have been so blind?" she asks during the break-up, when not too long ago she was totally enamored by *Prince Charming*. What we *see* in someone else is colored by our past relationships and experiences. We see only the mirrored reflection of what we hope, want, or expect to see, filtered through unmet attachment needs. *Mr. Wrong* is usually adept at *sniffing out* loneliness, insecurity, and unmet needs in order to target potential victims.

So who will benefit from these therapeutic stories about relationships? The stories may be used with anyone that experienced relational control or domestic violence (in a current or prior relationship) that wishes to address the *fallout* of the experienced trauma and move toward change. The stories are ideal for professional work in shelters, domestic violence treatment programs, school counseling, family and individual recovery programs, and mental health and may also be used for "self-help" homework. The stories are written at a 3rd- to 4th-grade level, and the somewhat humorous characters will appeal to readers of all ages. They may help older teens identify budding relationship problems in order to make better choices in their future relationships.

Childhood attachment experiences provide the building blocks for adult relationships. Siegel's (2003, p. 33) "interpersonal neurobiology approach" suggests that attachment relationships are likely to promote the development of the integrative capacities of the brain in enabling the acquisition of (these) emotional, cognitive, and interpersonal abilities. As a result, various types of maltreatment (emotional, physical, or sexual) in early life have the power to unravel affect regulation, attunement, and self-appraisal.

Abused and neglected children carry remnants of infant and childhood attachment into their dismissive, pre-occupied, or unresolved adult relationships (Dozier et al., 2001; Main, 1996; Siegel, 2003; Sfroufe et al., 1999; Zeanah et al., 2000). The way in which they do this appears to be through well-developed Internal Working Models and changed neurobiology (Ainsworth et al., 1978; Bowlby, 1988; Cozolino, 2006; Perry & Szalavitz, 2006; Siegel, 1999; Siegel and Hartzell, 2003; Thompson, 1999).

At a March 2010 trauma conference in Chicago, When Freud Meets Buddha, Bremner, Briere, and Ross (among others) discussed the ways in which child trauma impacts neurobiology, attachment, and adult relationships and suggested that mindfulness and trauma-focused therapy can remediate neurobiological and relational deficits. Many symptoms in grown-up abuse or neglect victims can be better understood within a trauma model, whereby adult behavior is driven by the need for survival, security, and being loved; and these are the core components of childhood attachment. Adult abuse victims yearn for a secure base, yet too often they recapitulate childhood experiences, raging at those that hurt them or becoming overly dependent to avoid rejection.

Research indicates that severe and/or chronic abuse affects the parts of the brain that think, plan, focus, and organize, that is, executive functioning domains (Briere, 2010; Bremner, 2010; Cozolino, 2006; McCollum, 2006; Schore, 2001; Siegel, 1999). Complex trauma impairs the pathways between the *thinking* and *feeling/sensing* brain areas, resulting in high arousal, poor affect modulation, and chronic stress response. The pathway of the heightened stress response (freeze, fight, or flee) eventually becomes automatic, like the deeply furrowed pathway of a swift down-flowing mountain stream (Perry & Svalavitz, 2006).

Chronic neglect also has a profound effect on child development. According to Colin Ross at the Freud Meets Buddha Conference (2010), the "invisibility" of neglect may be even more damaging than the pain of physical or sexual abuse in terms of self- and relationship development. When you are abused, at least you are *worthy* of someone's attention. A child ignored by those she loves has no "template" for healthy adult relationships, and "I'm not lovable" is indelibly stamped on her heart.

Women in maladaptive relationships differ widely in their view of relationship problems and their readiness for change. Some blame themselves and behave as if they *deserve punishment*, apologizing for their shortcomings. They vow to try harder and make fewer "mistakes" the next time. Others see that their partners are unreasonable, controlling, or even abusive, but can't yet contemplate making a change. Perhaps the risks of making a change (and there are many) outweigh the possible benefits. A woman in a volatile relationship fears for herself and her children; she may even be confronted by family pressure to maintain the "status quo."

In *Motivational Interviewing and Stages of Change in Intimate Partner Violence* (2009), editors Murphy and Maiuro publish a collection of essays about understanding and facilitating the change process in domestic violence perpetrators and their victims. The Transtheoretical Stages of Change Model of Prochaska & DiClemente (1983) is an excellent model for domestic violence intervention, and it provides the organizational structure for this book. This author agrees that only through practices such as Motivational Interviewing, where insight and decision-making arise from the client, will we make headway in reducing the incidence and impact of domestic violence. The book sections and stories are organized based on the goals and issues that tend to be present in each stage of change. The stories pose ideas that will challenge women to examine their attitudes, expectations, and behaviors within each stage of relational change.

According to the Transtheoretical Stages of Change Model (Prochaska & DiClemente, 1983; Prochaska & Velicer, 1997), persons with life problems or troublesome emotions/behavior may be in any of five stages: Pre-Contemplation, Contemplation, Preparation, Action, and Maintenance. As they go through the ebb and flow of the change process, individuals contemplate change (motivation to change and belief that the benefits outweigh the risks); make inner (attitudes and beliefs) and outward (behaviors) changes; and find ways to maintain change in the face of environmental stressors. It is important to recognize that the Stages of Change are not *set in stone*, in that women can move from one stage to another, back and forth, as they continuously weigh risks and benefits and confront life stressors.

A treatment provider needs to assess where a woman is in the change process before beginning intervention, since the types of change interventions are determined by the phase of the change process.

Persons in Pre-Contemplation do not see their behaviors as problematic and have no intention of making a change in the next six months. 50–60% of clients referred for treatment are in this phase, and many are uninformed or underinformed. In this phase, treatment increases awareness of the problem; points out discrepancies between how the person is functioning and how they would like to function; informs the person more about the value of treatment; and helps the person make an emotional shift if possible.

Once someone is Contemplating change, he or she recognizes that there is a problem but doesn't yet commit to or have a clear plan for changing. The person "sits on the fence" with his or her ambivalence, not sure how or when to move forward; so the therapist can help that individual consider the pros and cons of changing and instill hope about things improving after the change. It also can be helpful to provide educational materials that emphasize the discrepancy between current life situations and desired life situations.

In Preparation, the person has decided to change his or her life situation and behaviors *within a month*. That individual is taking small steps toward change but is not fully engaged in the change process. The therapist can assess if the person has the needed supports to make a change and the knowledge to carry it out. In this stage, therapists need to encourage the person's commitment to change, support self-efficacy, and help the person generate a plan and set action goals. Together they must identify barriers such as deficits in supports and skills; and the goals should be small and attainable. It is important to include the woman in her change plan, as the motivation to follow through will be greater.

Finally, there is Action. Someone in the Action phase of change has been making life changes between 1 and 180 days. It takes six months for a change to "solidify." The woman in this phase has developed new skills, is behaving differently, and she is motivated and enthusiastic. In this phase, the therapist provides positive verbal reinforcement, support for the belief that the client can sustain the change, and examples of specific new behaviors and attitudes that are observed.

After six months, the individual is usually committed to maintaining the new behavior and moves into the Maintenance phase. That person can see how life has changed and that he or she is thinking and behaving in new ways. At this stage, therapy might involve discussion about Relapse Prevention, and the client and therapist can review possible pitfalls of becoming overly confident and ignoring risk factors.

An unofficial stage, Relapse, occurs if the person resumes old behaviors. This can happen when life circumstances change, often at a time when a woman is under high stress, enters a new relationship, misses warning signs, or starts to question her prior judgment.

So how does the Stages of Change Model apply to women with relationship problems?

A woman in Pre-Contemplation is likely to be angry that the police have arrested her partner and may cover up what he has done and lie for him in court. She might agree to have her children placed in foster care rather than leave her partner. Another woman might justify, excuse, or minimize her partner's behavior.

A woman in Contemplation may repeatedly call the police then recant and return to her partner, ready to *try again* when he promises to change. Another woman in the Contemplation phase might come to a therapy intake, knowing she has a problem and upset by how her partner has treated her or her children, but not return for the next session.

A woman who is in Preparation plans to make a significant change within the next month. She has a plan and knows the steps she needs to go through to carry out that plan. Her plan may be to enter treatment and to take out an EPO the next time her partner assaults her. Or perhaps she has a plan to leave her partner—she has made contact with the local domestic violence shelter and consulted with a provider about legal and financial issues. She also might have arranged to stay with a friend or relative or put a downpayment on a house or apartment.

Those in the Action phase have moved past the planning phase and are acting on their plans. They have made decisions and taken decisive action toward safety. They may have moved to the shelter or taken out an EPO and asked the partner to leave. In the Action phase, women show good cognitive understanding of their relational problems but need encouragement to hang in there through financial difficulties and sleepless nights filled with loneliness, nightmares, and anxiety.

At any stage, strong, confusing emotions and ambivalence impede the change process. The loss of financial support can be daunting; and unmet needs for affection and dependency exert a strong pull, like the pull of the ocean's undercurrents. It is easy to escape the pull close to shore, but a strong riptide can catch you in its grip and pull you to deeper water. You are over your head and drowning before you know it.

There can be "blind spots" at any stage of treatment. Women in Pre-Contemplation may justify, minimize, or excuse a partner's behavior. A woman may terminate treatment prematurely, before she is ready, unaware that it takes time for change to "solidify" and that circumstances (life events or new relationships) may pull her out of recovery into relapse.

It is reasonable to ask what constitutes an unhealthy relationship. Relational harm lies on a continuum, with "small" emotional hurts at one end of the continuum (for example, hurtful behaviors that make others "flinch"); and severe domestic violence or death at the other. Along the continuum are many types of harmful behaviors, such as excessive control or intimidation, verbal threats, disdainful criticism, substance abuse, and infidelity.

Developmental Psychopathology and Family Process (Cummings et al., 2000) describes developmental pathways, whereby multiple causes can result in a single outcome (equifinality) and multiple outcomes can result from a common cause (multifinality). Women with relationship difficulties are not "one size fits all" in terms of their developmental pathways; in fact, biological, psychological, cultural, social, and environmental factors interact to create pathways that allow some women to become resilient survivors while putting other women at risk of violence. No one factor or factors ensures relational health or victimization.

The risk factors associated with domestic violence are many: insecure attachment, depression or anxiety, personality disorders, substance abuse, low self-esteem, poor mood regulation, external locus of control, learned helplessness, witnessing relational violence as children, or prior abuse or neglect. Abused women often grew up in families with traditional gender roles, parental substance abuse, and marital/partner infidelity; as a result, they later struggle with role boundaries and trust. Briere and Jordan (2009) discuss the many ways that childhood trauma may impact adult functioning. Yet some women that grew up in abusive or neglectful families outsmart the "riptide," finding the resources, community supports, and means to live healthy relational lives

Obviously, growing up in a "less than" culture provides limited exposure to appropriate relationships. Women that are drawn to "bad boys" and push away "nice guys," who try to nurture or care for them, later weep or rage with anger when their partners are unfaithful, violent, or rejecting. They see abandonment as "proof" that *true love* is only a fairy tale. A woman used to relational violence may experience a "magnetic" pull to the one man in the room that is least likely to support her growth and wholeness. It is a matter of "fit and familiarity." We all gravitate to partners that "fit with" our past; ones that recapitulate prior relational experiences and reinforce our definitions of "self."

To be able to *outsmart the riptide* and choose healthy relationships, a woman needs first to develop strong, positive self-regard and to access or develop resources for self-sufficiency. Most victims of domestic violence are quite dependent on their partners for economic support, so they require case management services in order to access affordable housing and gainful employment. Once they have the means to be self-sufficient, victims of violence benefit from intensive treatment for them and their families.

Treatment for domestic violence victims needs to include problem-solving, decision-making, safety plans, coping skills, mood management, self-soothing, mindfulness, reducing avoidance and agitation, attachment remediation, and relationship recovery. The problem with traditional interventions for domestic violence is that the "cookie cutter" approaches used in many settings are, for the most part, psycho-educational, lacking psychotherapeutic emphasis on core attachment and personality deficits.

Each story in this book focuses on a different relational issue in the change process. The mindfulness meditations in the appendix parallel issues in some of the stories. The author believes that metaphor and mindfulness seed change from the inside-out, and unless women change their needs and perceptions from the inside-out, they are likely to return to their former lives when treatment, often court-ordered, is completed.

The stories in this book will ring familiar for many victims of domestic violence. They are not meant to be any sort of "cure," but they may facilitate the healing process. When metaphorical stories are added to group or individual treatment, and mindfulness meditation is introduced, women are more likely to be able to alter core schemas and "calm down" their over-aroused neurobiology. Therapeutic metaphor opens eyes and springboards clients into new relational territory and honest discussion. It is much easier to see one's own issues in someone else's story.

It is important to point out that metaphorical stories may be used within any evidence-based model of therapeutic change. A number of expert clinicians and writers (Burns, 2007; O'Hanlon, 1992; Zeig, 2008) have proposed that metaphorical stories have the capacity to evoke an "aha," seed possibility, and propel change. Treatments in which metaphor has been used include Trauma-Focused CBT (TF-CBT) and other Cognitive Behavioral Treatment (CBT), Relapse Prevention & Recovery Dynamics, Cognitive Processing Therapy, Schema Therapy, Narrative Therapy, Interpersonal Psychotherapy, Dialectical Behavior Therapy, Acceptance & Commitment Therapy, and Mindfulness-Based Stress Reduction.

Why is storytelling, an age-old tradition in all cultures, so compelling? Stories, and metaphors, teach, arouse emotion, promote insight, and reduce avoidance and defensiveness. Stories allow women to "see themselves" or their situations through a special lens, that is, a story's theme or characters— this allows *exposure* with some psychological distance.

A process for using stories and metaphor in treatment is as follows:

1. Therapist creates a relaxing atmosphere: pillows or beanbag chair on floor; a comfortable rocker or recliner; and perhaps a sound machine with good background "noise."
2. Therapist selects a pertinent story, often one that has a character with whom the client will identify; or a story with a theme that parallels the client's current issues or goals. When using the stories within a TF-CBT format, therapist may select a story specifically for the purpose of Psycho-education, Relaxation, Affect modulation, Cognitive restructuring, Trauma narrative work, In vivo exposure, Conjoint work on parent-child relationship, or Ensuring safety. Or the therapist may select a story to help the client carry out an activity within a particular stage of change, such as the risk-benefit analysis needed during Contemplation.
3. Therapist asks client if it is OK to read a story. Simply say, "I would like to read you a story. It reminded me of you and I think you will relate to it."
4. Therapist reads the story to the client. Or, if in a group, each group member may take a turn reading.
5. Therapist notes which parts of the story elicit bemused head-shaking, smiling, facial emotions, agitation, etc.
6. When finished, if client does not spontaneously remark on something in the story, ask client neutral questions such as, "What came up for you?" or "What did you think?"
7. Client will often say, "That sounds like me" or "Is that supposed to be my partner?"
8. After the story is read, therapist and client discuss what comes up, with the therapist helping client draw parallels with his or her life, and assigning homework activity based on the story theme.

Other clients may wish to take the stories home, read on their own, mull over them or journal about them, and then bring back points of interest to the therapy. Frequently the metaphors stir up stories of the past and help women process issues formerly avoided.

Adult relationships are so often the recapitulation of unmet childhood attachment needs. Early relational experiences shape one's core schemas and sense of self. How we are treated in the first few years of life becomes the foundation for whether we trust others, feel "good enough," believe we are lovable, expect rejection, anticipate maltreatment, or feel significant.

Metaphorical stories allow clients to safely experience sensations, emotions, and memories that might otherwise be avoided or experienced as overwhelming. In part because the stories are "childlike" and "simple," they invite the client to leave the realm of rational thought and move into right-brain emotional and sensory processing. Stories tend to be emotionally provoking; and emotions judged to be unacceptable (shame, regret, envy, fear, rage, doubt, and guilt) are more easily accessed through metaphor than by direct methods. In reflecting on the characters in the stories and the themes in the meditation narratives, women recognize truths about themselves and experience an "aha" and familiarity that springboards them toward change.

For years, Ericksonian therapists have been using trance work to facilitate change. For this writer, the concepts of "mindfulness" and "meditation," and the states that they elicit, are similar to states of trance, self-hypnosis, or guided imagery. Some of the components of EMDR resemble hypnotic trance induction; and the mindfulness of DBT results in a focused state of consciousness. Whatever you call them, deeply focused states that carry participants into right-brain, emotional, and sensory areas of the brain are helpful and restorative in the change process.

Body-mind work (Van der Kolk) is helpful as women process traumatic experiences and integrate the right (emotional) and left (cognitive) brain pathways. Mindfulness practices allow women to "tune into" their experiences and tolerate strong emotions without over- or underreacting. According to Bremner and his colleagues, who presented on the use of mindfulness in trauma intervention (Freud Meets Buddha, March 2010), trauma results in neurobiological changes. Bremner's work at Emory University on PTSD indicates that trauma impairs memory (hippocampus), concentration and attention, executive functioning and cognitive processing, and emotional regulation (limbic overarousal). Medications such as SSRIs, clonidine, or propranolol help reduce arousal and dissociation; and trauma-focused therapy results in neurobiological recovery. The approaches presented at Freud Meets Buddha (Yoga, meditation, mindfulness, adult attachment development, and cognitive restructuring) paralleled some of the elements of Trauma-Focused CBT of Cohen and her colleagues and stressed the need for Integrative Therapy like that proposed by Briere and Langtree (2008) in their guide for those multiply traumatized. Integrative therapy allows women to examine the connections among emotions, thoughts, and life experiences, while decreasing the arousal associated with trauma responding. It is encouraging that integrative treatment with mindfulness components can result in neurobiological changes that were not formerly believed possible, such as hippocampus regrowth and new cell growth that allows better executive functioning and emotional processing.

In 2008, Praissman reviewed the Mindfulness-Based Stress Reduction (MBSR) program established by Jon Kabat-Zinn at the University of Massachusetts Medical School and found it to be promising for a variety of conditions. The benefits of mindfulness practices include an increase in the body's immune system's ability to ward off disease, a shift from right prefrontal cortex (associated with anxiety, depression, and aversion) to the left prefrontal cortex (associated with happiness), and a reduction in perceived stress.

Jon Kabat-Zinn has defined mindfulness as a moment-to-moment non-evaluative awareness of all available affective states, physical sensations, sensations, imagery, and thoughts without rejection, judgment, questioning, or aversion. It is quite non-deliberate and observational. Jon Kabat-Zinn has also said that the principles of mindfulness, on which MBSR is based, have been most clearly articulated by persons in Buddhist traditions; but the program itself is not spiritually based.

Ruth Baer has edited an excellent collection of articles about mindfulness and acceptance-based treatments for children, adolescents, and adults in *Mindfulness-Based Treatment Approaches: Clinician's Guide to Evidence Base and Applications (Practical Resources for the Mental Health Professional)*. She includes a chapter by Rathus, Cavuoto, and Passarelli who succinctly write about the effectiveness of DBT (Dialectical Behavior Therapy) in the treatment of intimate partner violence. It is this author's contention that mindfulness-based interventions will be an important part of any program that intends to address the interpersonal and mood regulation difficulties *associated with* domestically violent relationships. This author will not reinvent the wheel of mindfulness; rather, she directs the reader to other works and programs that are mindfulness-based. However, the author has written a collection of narratives for Guided Contemplation, ideal for beginning or ending sessions focused on domestic violence or relationship issues. The narratives in the appendix are to be used for stress reduction and objective, non-judgmental self-examination. Their themes parallel the themes of the stories, thus they also have the capacity to "cement" some of the concepts introduced during the session, guiding the reader toward Radical Acceptance.

Hopefully, these stories and narratives will be incorporated into trauma work in a variety of settings. I encourage you to use the stories and narratives in group, individual, or family therapy with those that seek relational recovery and to individualize your interventions so as to help women and their loved ones better navigate the stages of change. Each story comes from the life story of a real client; therefore what has been effective once may well be effective again—and again.

Part I

STORIES FOR PRE-CONTEMPLATION

The stories included in this section are meant to raise awareness and tweak emotion. Women in Pre-Contemplation do not yet recognize that their behaviors or the behaviors of their partners are problematic. They are often referred through the court for domestic violence batterers or victims groups and they lack awareness that their lives could be improved by a change in behavior. Their children may have been removed by Child Protective Services or there may be a protective order prohibiting contact between the parents until they complete "anger management" or domestic violence psycho-education. What they want to do is satisfy the court order and get back to "life as usual."

To help women move from this stage of change to the next (Contemplation), interventions must raise some sort of dissonance that helps the client see there is a problem. Dissonance is when you begin to feel uncomfortable due to a discrepancy between how you want to perceive yourself and real life events that challenge that perception. You may no longer be able to lie, distort, avoid, or defend when facts are staring you in the face. The facts may ruffle your comfort level and point to relationship problems.

The characters in the stories that follow are initially blind to the need for change. According to the Stages of Change model, 50–60% of clients are in this stage when they are referred or court-ordered to treatment. They may be underinformed or uninformed, so the purpose of the treatment at this stage is to raise consciousness about their life circumstances. Stories for this stage of change allow the therapist to move the client emotionally or provide education about intimate partner violence and cross-generational patterns. Intervention at this stage can reduce defensiveness so that women begin to see relationship problems and begin contemplating change.

1

Investing in Others

Relationships

The quality of infant and childhood attachment affects a person's capacity for attunement empathy, trust, healthy separation, and individuation (Bowlby, 1988; Cozolino, 2006; Siegel, 1999; Siegel & Hartzell, 2003). During childhood, reliable adults are supposed to provide a secure base so that children eventually become autonomous and trust others. Children who grow up without a secure base often become adults with Dismissive, Preoccupied, or Unresolved attachments (Siegel & Hartzell, 2003; Main, 1996).

Dismissive adults may relate to others as if they are expendable or interchangeable. People may "all look the same," almost like "apples in a basket." Dismissive individuals try to meet their needs in egocentric, self-centered ways. Dismissive men lack the capacity to see women as persons with their own feelings, thoughts, and needs; and may stereotype women as only good for sex, housekeeping, or raising children. They may view women as possessions or objects. Dismissive women may "use" men as "meal tickets" or "providers," taking advantage of their financial generosity, but not risking emotional intimacy with their partners.

Someone with a Dismissive Attachment is likely to have superficial, stereotyped relationships and blame others for his or her own relationship deficits. One woman announced in group that she had been with about 30 partners in the prior two years. Each had been, for her, a source of financial support, superficial emotional dependency, and sexual gratification. None particularly stood out, as she did not allow herself the time to really know them before she became involved. The story that follows, *Apples in a Basket*, introduces clients to these concepts and opens up discussion.

APPLES IN A BASKET

John had a large basket of apples in his bedroom, and he went through apples like a hot, thirsty dog laps up water.

"They all look alike," John often said. "Apples in a basket . . . They're all red. They're all round. They all have that short little stem. They're all dimpled on the bottom. How boring . . ."

Each time John reached into the apple basket, he imagined that *maybe this time* he would find the perfect apple. He would go to the basket, look for the prettiest, shiniest apple, pick it up, take a bite or two, but no, it was just like all the others. John then threw the apple away, ready to move on to the next.

John also had a wastebasket full of discarded, thrown-away apples in his bedroom. Each apple in the wastebasket had a brown spot where John had taken a bite.

No apple held John's interest for very long. That was just how he was—he got bored very quickly. And John kept hoping to find the *perfect* apple.

One lazy afternoon, John lay on his bed watching TV in his bedroom. He lived at his parents' home, without rent, and he had the whole lower level to himself. He was trying to find a job. As usual, John was bored.

"Knock-knock."

"Come in," said John.

The door opened and in walked John's dad.

John and his dad talked for a few minutes about how he was doing in his job hunt.

"Hang in there, John," said his dad. "It's a tough job market right now. I'm sure you'll find something if you keep at it. I'm off to work now—see you later."

As he was leaving John's room, John's dad saw the wastebasket full of partly eaten apples. He paused.

"John, why are you taking just one or two bites and then tossing each apple? It seems such a waste."

"Dad," said John. "I'm looking for the perfect apple. But these apples in a basket are all the same. So after one or two bites I'm bored. Sometimes I think I'll never find the perfect apple."

John's dad scratched his head. "John," he replied, "There's no such thing as a perfect apple—and no two apples are the same."

"What do you mean?" asked John.

"You might want to pick out two apples you threw in the trash, John," said his dad, "and take a closer look."

John picked two apples out of his trash basket.

"What do you see?" asked his dad.

"Both of the apples are red, shiny, and round," answered John.

"Look a little closer," said his dad.

John looked a little closer.

"Each has one bite out of it," John replied.

"Look a little closer," suggested his dad again.

John looked a little closer.

John said, "Well, one is a little less round."

"Look even closer," his dad reminded.

John looked very closely at the apples and noticed differences he had not seen before. One apple's stem was bent to the side. It had a brown spot near the stem and two dimples on the bottom. The other apple had no stem at all. It had no brown spots, was a deeper red color, had no dimples on the bottom, and was not as big as the other apple.

"OK, Dad," said John. "I can see differences in these two apples. But what is the point?"

John's dad owned a winery where he made many types of wine.

His dad said, "It's a little like fine wine, son. No two bottles of fine wine taste the same. A wine taster takes just a mouthful at a time. He breathes in the aroma, enjoys the rich color, and appreciates the subtle flavors. He savors the wine. Only a glutton would gulp down a fine wine or take one sip and pour the rest down the drain."

John replied, "I don't see what that has to do with apples."

"The point is that the problem is not with the apples," said John's dad. "It's with you. You seem to be in too much of a hurry to appreciate each apple's flaws and beauty. One apple may be a little more tart and another a little more sweet. Eat one at a time, enjoy it and finish it before you start on another."

John had been bored with apples for a long time and he had to think about what his dad had said.

"OK," he said, "So let's say the problem isn't with the apples, it's with me. What do I do about that?"

"It's up to you," said his dad. "Do what you want, but don't blame the apples. Carpe Diem—Seize the Day!"

John took in his father's words. John had been bored with many things in his life, such as his job, his dating life, and his friends. So maybe his boredom was more about him and things he needed to change in himself. Maybe he needed to change how he thought about apples *and* how he thought about his life.

THE BOTTOM LINE: There is no perfect apple!

FOOD FOR THOUGHT QUESTIONS

1. How are you like John?
2. What advice would you give John to help him appreciate each apple?
3. How are apples like relationships?

2

The Extent of the Problem

"She knows she would be better off without him—why doesn't she leave?" asks her friend. But it is not that simple. Staying or leaving depends on the magnitude of the problem and involves risks, losses, and benefits.

There are a number of reasons why women stay in hurtful relationships. A woman's blind spots may prevent her from seeing anything wrong with how she is being treated. She may lack resources such as transportation and housing and not have the means of supporting herself. Some women have become isolated and are unaware of community services. Sometimes staying in a troubled relationship is a matter of convenience or familiarity. I remember a woman who said, "I need help with the bills and he does the home and auto repairs. Having him around is better than being alone."

Change is hard—it takes time, energy, and perseverance. Some changes are harder and more risky than others. A colleague once said, "A woman trying to 'keep peace' in a domestically violent relationship is flying in the eye of a hurricane." If she moves *with* the storm, she can stay within her small circle of safety, yet she will soon become exhausted and find it difficult to maintain that position. She will risk her life if she tries to move outside the circle of safety, but perhaps that is the only way for her to really survive in the long run. It takes great courage and a little luck to fly *through* the destructive winds and rain to get to a point outside the hurricane's path. As she makes her move, the storm may destroy her but she is willing to die trying. A woman needs to be at the point in her life where she knows that the storm is dangerous and that she might prefer seeking security.

HOW BAD IS THE HOLE?

Cheryl Chimpanzee had once again fallen in the mud hole in the middle of the path that led to her favorite tree. That tree had a great swinging vine, and she loved swinging in the tree with her children and partner George. The tree's thick branches extended over the river, and the vines were great for going, "Ah-a-ah-a-ah!" right before you swung out and dropped in the water.

The only part of Cheryl's day that was not fun was falling in the mud hole. It was a fairly deep mud hole, filled with muddy water, and it hurt when she landed in the bottom. But every day, Cheryl fell in the hole. It was too big to swing across and there were thorn bushes on either side of it. "Oh well," Cheryl figured. "I guess that's just something I have to put up with if I want to get to my favorite tree. The hole's not so bad."

Cheryl was curious, though. George never had mud on him. He arrived at the tree each day with his black, hairy muscular body looking just as clean and handsome as when he left their home. Cheryl didn't want to seem stupid, but she finally had decided to ask George how he avoided the mud hole. The path she took was the only path she knew that led to the river and the swinging tree.

That morning, Cheryl arrived at their swinging tree, muddy as usual. She swung over to George and said, "Can I ask you a stupid question, honey?"

George hugged Cheryl, pounded his fists on his broad hairy chest, and grinned as he said, "You can ask this big, strong King of the Jungle any questions you like. There aren't any stupid questions."

Cheryl replied, "Oh thanks, George." She laughed, too, because George was such a show-off. He liked to show her how big and strong he was. He said he would always "take care of" her, but they both knew Cheryl was perfectly capable of taking care of herself. She took care of the children, picked bananas each day, and paid all the bills. All George did was swing around the trees and pound his hairy chest! Still, he was a wonderful guy and she loved him with all her heart.

"George," said Cheryl. "Maybe you have noticed that I'm always muddy when I arrive at the swinging tree?"

"No honey," said George. "I hadn't really noticed. Why?"

Cheryl smiled. It was just like George to not notice. After all, he didn't notice the banana peels he dropped on the floor of their bedroom or the cap he left off the toothpaste.

Cheryl explained, "I'm all muddy when I get here, because I fall in the mud hole on the path from our home to the river. But you aren't muddy when you get here. How do you avoid the mud hole?"

"What mud hole are you talking about?" George asked. "What path?"

"You know, George—the path from our home that goes through the woods and ends up at this tree and the river."

George hung his head.

"Actually, Cheryl," he admitted. "I don't take that path. Awhile back I found another path that goes from our home to the river by way of the berry patch. I like to stop for a snack on my way to the swimming hole."

George added, scratching his head, "Cheryl, if the path you take has a big mud hole in the middle of it, why do you take that path? If you fall in the mud hole every time you take that path, one of these days you're going to get hurt."

"Oh, George," replied Cheryl. "I can take a little bump on the head . . . Or a sprained ankle . . . or a few stitches in my head when I hit it on a rock. . . ."

"Cheryl!" exclaimed George. "You told me you fell on a rock when you were swinging on a vine!"

"I didn't want to worry you, George," said Cheryl, hanging her head and peering up at George with tears in her eyes.

"But why do you keep taking the same path if you know you risk getting hurt?" he asked again.

Cheryl explained, "George, I'm such a creature of habit! That's the only path to the river I know, and I don't like to explore. I might get lost if I went any other way. You know how much I hate change, and the hole is no major problem."

George put his arm around Cheryl and said, "Honey, any hole is a problem if you keep falling in. I'll show you the new path if you decide to give it a try; then you can avoid falling in the mud hole each day. I wish you had brought it up sooner!"

"Oh, George," murmured Cheryl, "I knew that if I brought it up you would try to convince me to take a new path. I wasn't ready to hear that. But you are *soooo* persuasive, honey, and I will consider your advice," smiled Cheryl, batting her eyes to make him think he was *really something* as she gave him a big hug.

Cheryl knew George was right. She was tired of falling in the same old hole on the same old path. It might be time to try a new pathway. Who knows why it took Cheryl so long to speak up and ask for help, because after all, even a creature of habit is capable of making one small change.

THE BOTTOM LINE: No hole is too small!

FOOD FOR THOUGHT QUESTIONS

1. How are you like Cheryl?
2. How would life improve if you considered a new path?
3. What "bad habits" have you had trouble changing? What one step could you take to move in a new direction?
4. What is your "hole?" How big is it?

3

Tuning In

Parent-Child Interaction

Some victims inadvertently put themselves and their children at risk by *tuning out* potential danger. Children are naturally curious and trusting and they can get hurt when their parents ignore, avoid, or do not pay attention to risks in the environment. Women with unprocessed trauma issues often miss "warning signs" in new relationships, even those that are controlling, dismissive, or demeaning. A woman may unwittingly select partners that have the same characteristics as prior perpetrators, thus continuing the cycle of abuse.

There are a number of ways that a woman may put her children at risk. For example, if the mother dissociated off the memory of her own abuse, she may not "see" what is happening to her child, even if there are clear warning signs. A mother who took care of herself and her siblings when she was young may think it's OK to put an older child in charge. A mother with financial problems may leave her children with non-reputable caretakers. And if the mother is using mind-altering substances (to numb feelings or self-medicate trauma symptoms), she may not be alert or aware enough to notice risks; or invite untrustworthy *friends* into her home. A mother with mental illness may misperceive what is going on in her relationships and in her home. And a grown-up victim may unwittingly "set up" her children to be abused by avoiding sex with her partner through the hours she works.

One mother in particular had allowed her children, ages 4 and 6, to visit the home of an older man in her neighborhood, which resulted in sexual abuse. "He liked kids and seemed nice," she said, "Especially little girls. You therapists always think the worst of people." She had missed all the warning signs. The story that follows encourages women to do what they need to do to sharpen their focus and protect their children from harm.

20

SHARPEN YOUR FOCUS

A woman and her friend were lounging outside on the second-story back deck, talking about which restaurant they would eat at that day. They had smoked a joint together and were on their third Cosmo martini. The woman was squinting as she watched her child play on the grass below, next to the sidewalk leading to the garage.

Her friend asked, "Why are you squinting?"

"My glasses are a little out of focus," the woman replied.

"Yah, right," smiled her friend. "I'm sure it's the glasses. It's certainly not the reefer or the Cosmos."

"No, really," protested the woman. "It's the glasses."

Her friend commented, "Well I'm sure the joint and the drinks don't help any. Didn't you just get new glasses last week?"

"Yes, I got new glasses. But I'm not wearing them yet," said the mother. "I like these old glasses."

Her friend replied, "Those old glasses are three years old."

"Yes," said the woman. "But I'm used to them and they're comfortable. I'm not sure I want to wear the new glasses."

"If you got new glasses, why don't you want to wear them? You're half-blind with the old ones. Remember last week, when you almost hit the guy in the crosswalk?"

"I saw the guy in the crosswalk," the woman replied. "I just wasn't paying attention."

"But why are you still wearing your old glasses?" asked her friend.

"It's complicated," said the woman with a smile, as she stretched out on her lawn chair. "I don't really mind not being able to see things. The old frames are really comfortable. It's like that saying, 'What I can't see won't hurt me.' And you know how much I hate change . . ."

"You need to see what's really going on around you," argued her friend. "You're a mother now. I don't know how you can keep an eye on the baby unless you wear your new glasses."

At that moment, the two-year-old started climbing up the steep wooden stairs that led to the second-story deck.

"Look at that!" said the friend.

"What?" the woman asked.

"You better go get the baby. He's going to get hurt."

"Where is he?" asked the woman, squinting. "I can't see him."

"He's down there below us, climbing up the steep wooden stairs."

The woman replied, "Oh, he won't get hurt; he's a good climber."

"Wanting something to be true won't make it true," remarked her friend. "He's too little to climb without help. You need to keep an eye on him."

"I don't think anything bad will happen to him," said the woman. "But since you are so concerned, I'll go get him."

"It's about time," the friend muttered under her breath.

"If you say so," the woman said in a lazy voice. She stood up, wobbled over to the top of the stairs, and grabbed onto the deck rail. As she moved carefully down the steps, the baby saw her coming, grinned, and started climbing down the steps backwards, away from her.

Then "EEEEEEEEEEE!" went a loud scream. The baby had tripped trying to go back down the steps and was now hanging off the edge, holding on to the rail with one tight little fist, his feet dangling in mid air ten feet up from the ground below.

The woman shouted, "Oh my God, don't let go!" and stumbled down the steps to the baby. Her friend was right behind her. Each woman grabbed a chubby arm and together they pulled the baby up to safety. The mother cradled the child in her arms, while he clung to her and cried with gut-shaking sobs.

"He's OK," said the mother to her friend. "I told you nothing bad would happen."

"Are you kidding?" asked the friend in amazement. "Your baby almost fell ten feet off the stairs to the sidewalk below, and you say 'nothing bad happened'?"

It was like she woke up from a deep sleep. The woman suddenly realized what might have happened if the baby had not held on. Her composure crumbled and she burst into tears. Her friend took the baby from her saying, "Come on, all's well that ends well. Let's go back in the house now and go to lunch."

They climbed the steps and went inside with the baby, who was once again calm and smiling as he babbled at his mother. The woman called a cab to take them to lunch, as she realized that neither she nor her friend were in any condition to drive.

She said to her friend, "Just a minute. There's something I need to do before we leave for lunch."

She reached into her purse, pulled out a glasses case, and switched her old glasses for the new.

"Here," she said as she handed the old glasses to her friend. "Let's donate these to a local charity, so I won't be tempted to put them back on. They may have been OK three years ago, but not anymore."

She added, "You were right, you know. I'm a mother now. I have to be able to see what's really going on."

You might think that this change was rather sudden, but the woman had been thinking about whether to change her glasses since the day she brought home the new ones. She had contemplated long enough— the close call had been a wake-up call. It was time for her to make the change. You might also point out that she needed to change her lifestyle a little, now that she was a mother, and you would be making a good point. After all, once you're a mother, your "me-time" becomes "we-time," whether you like it or not.

THE BOTTOM LINE: Sharpen your focus!

FOOD FOR THOUGHT QUESTIONS

1. How do you spend "me-time" and "we-time"?
2. In what area of your life do you find yourself making the most excuses to others?
3. In what ways do you still act younger than your age?
4. What is one thing you could do to sharpen your focus?

4

Repeated Exposure to Domestic Violence

Children and their mothers are often exposed to repeated episodes of domestic violence, and some end up in shelters or spend hours developing safety plans. Which neighbor's house can be the safe place? Where in the house can they hide? What can they use as a weapon the next time their dad attacks their mother? Who can they call if things get out of control? Who will take care of them if their mother is killed?

Living in such a stressful home is like walking on eggshells, with family members waiting for the next tsunami, or earthquake, or hurricane to strike. The family never knows when the next episode of violence will erupt, and "for the sake of the children" the mother keeps letting her partner/husband return home. As everyone knows, "children need their father."

The mother does not realize the impact of domestic violence on her own coping resources least of all the impact on her children. She avoids looking at how violence has changed her and her family. It is painful for children to carry the burden of watching their mother repeatedly hurt "for their sake." Children love their parents, but they cannot cope with that kind of stress.

One mother in particular had returned to her abusive, substance-dependent husband numerous times throughout her children's lives. She depended on him and kept believing he would change. She did not realize that wishing for something to be true does not make it true. Each time he returned, the abuse grew worse—at one point he cut his wrist in front of his daughter, and the blood that sprayed her has left an indelible memory. The children began to display symptoms of PTSD. Finally, the mother was able to see the damage that had been done to her children. The following story is a somewhat humorous portrayal of one such mother and how her children convince her to stop exposing them to recurring violence.

TRICK OR TREAT

It was a full-moon Halloween night. A mother dressed in a black witch's costume held the hands of her two children, the moon's glow casting shadows around them. The smallest child was in a clown costume, and the oldest was dressed as a ninja. Their breath smoked in the cold air, and they shivered at the sight of what lay just ahead. It was a large shingled house, foreboding in the moonlight, with a witch's cauldron simmering on the porch and orange candles flickering in each window.

The mother said, "Come on, let's go there next," pointing at the creepy-looking, house. "Haunted House," said the sign out front.

"No way, Mom," said the smaller child, pulling back. "I'm not going in the haunted house this year. And I can't believe you would ask us to go back there, after what happened last year."

"Nonsense," said the mother. "It was not that bad last year. Oh, I admit it was a little scary, but we should give it another try. After all, Halloween only comes once a year."

"Mom," said the older child, "Every year we say we don't want to go in the haunted house. And every year you tell us it won't be as bad this year and then it turns out to be at least as bad or even worse."

The clown's nose wrinkled up with disgust. "Remember the worms last year? Mom, you told us they were just sour candy and to eat them, but they turned out to be real worms! They made me puke!"

"Well, they didn't *look like* real worms in the dark," answered the mother. "And they didn't taste *that bad*. The man at the haunted house promised not to do the worms again."

The ninja argued, "Every year he makes promises—but he doesn't keep them. And he's *really* mean. The torture chamber he set up had real torture. He put me on a rack and stretched me until I cried!"

The mom grew silent, caught off-guard by the vivid visual memory that popped into her head—of her daughter crying on the rack in the dark, musty room. But she quickly pushed the memory back down, regained her perky attitude and said, "No pain, no gain, I always say."

"But a haunted house shouldn't have things in it that *really* hurt you!" retorted the ninja.

"Well of course I didn't want you to get hurt," said the mother, "but that's all in the past now, so you should just forget about it. Maybe you could pretend it was all just a bad dream."

"But it wasn't a dream," said the child. "The worms and the torture were REAL!"

"I know, I know," replied the mother. "But the man said he was really sorry for hurting you and he promised not to do it again. Can't we give him another chance?"

The children didn't trust the man to keep his promise, but they loved their mother and didn't want to disappoint her. They knew how much she loved Halloween. So they followed her down the sidewalk to the house . . .

As they stepped on the doormat, a deep scary voice said, "Welcome to the haunted house. Enter at your own risk." The clown and the ninja grabbed each other's hands and huddled together.

"Creak," went the front door as it opened. The family crept inside the dark house. "Slam!" went the front door as it closed behind them.

A man appeared out of nowhere, his face lit up by his glow-in-the-dark vampire shirt. "Happy Halloween and welcome," he said as he held out a tray of chocolate chip cookies.

The clown cautiously took a cookie and took a bite. "OMG!" the child shouted and spit out the bite. "What is in this cookie?"

"Oh chocolate chips and just a little dog food to add crunch." He paused, "But the plate was under my hamster cage, so I hope nothing else fell on the cookies." He raised his eyebrows and smiled.

"Mom, the bad stuff is starting already. We need to leave," said the ninja.

"Sweetie," said the mother, "it was an accident if anything fell out of the hamster cage on the cookies—not his fault at all. Let's see the rest of the house."

One room at a time, the family made their way through the haunted house. They were really nervous, because they didn't know what was coming.

The next room had a bowl full of fake cut-off fingers made out of cookie dough and red food coloring. The children looked them over carefully, and the ninja picked one up and took a bite. "Mmmmm, this is good!" she said in surprise.

"See," said the mother, "that cookie is just fine." They all munched on cookies as they moved on to the next room, where a round table held a plate of sparkling witch-hat cupcakes. Just as they entered the room, all three had a sudden need to use the bathroom.

"What is going on?" the children asked the man, sure that he was responsible.

"Oh, that must be the Ex-Lax that I put in the fingers," he said with a snicker as he gave another mean smile.

The children grabbed their mother by the hand and pulled her toward the door. "Mom, we're leaving now and we are *never* coming back. How many times do you have to put us through this crap before you understand it's not going to change?"

As they pulled their mother along, she said, "Just a minute. I want to ask him what he put on the cupcakes that makes them sparkle."

The man heard the mother and said, "Before you go, you might like to know that the cupcake sparkles are fragments of my favorite wine glass. Nothing sparkles quite as nice as shattered crystal."

The mother gasped, visibly angry, finally aware that the man had endangered her children. She said with outrage, "That is the last straw. I talked my children into coming back to your haunted house and gave you another chance. You promised not to do mean things this year. My children were right. You can't be trusted."

"That's true," he said slyly. "I did promise. But I didn't promise to *keep* my promise . . . And I never asked you to trust me."

At that, the family left the haunted house and went straight home. The mother made some hot chocolate for her children and then sat down in the family room to talk with them.

She said, "I let you both down. I don't know what came over me, to take you back to a place where you were hurt in the past. I shouldn't have trusted that man, and I should have listened to you. I am so sorry—and I hope you will forgive me. We will never go back there."

"Are you sure?" asked the children. Sometimes their mother had trouble following through.

"I am absolutely sure. That man is not going to change, and wanting it to be better won't make it better. I know that I hurt you by taking you back there, year after year."

The children sighed in relief. Thank goodness their mother had finally realized that sometimes you have to do the right thing, no matter how much you want to do something else.

THE BOTTOM LINE: The treats aren't worth the tricks!

FOOD FOR THOUGHT QUESTIONS

1. Give an example of a time you put your needs or wants before those of your children.
2. Give an example of a time when you didn't listen closely to someone else's feelings or concerns.
3. What is something you have done more than once, knowing it was hurting you or someone else?

5

Self-Destructive Behavior

Some swimmers drown without ever escaping the riptide. They fight against it as they are carried farther and farther out to sea. But those that escape it usually don't go back, at least not intentionally. When they return to the sea, they move quickly to the side as soon as they feel the strong pull of the current and they avoid swimming when they are warned to stay out of the water on "high riptide" days. Most women do everything they can to avoid or escape riptides.

But there are those that go back to the life-and-death situation of domestic violence (DV). You might think that only a fool or a self-destructive martyr would intentionally go back into the riptide. But some women get used to drama and risk, and become *addicted* to the pain or excitement. Without a dominant, controlling man around, such women feel helpless, lonely, bored, or depressed, especially if they are in recent recovery from drugs or alcohol. After all, living in a violent relationship is a little like getting high or self-cutting. Fear turns on the "fight or flight" centers of the brain with a real "adrenaline rush," and the unpredictable nature of DV keeps the person in a perpetual fast lane. It is like a bad habit she does not know how to break.

Persons that work with victims of DV need to recognize the signs of self-destruction. Those in the substance abuse field speak of "hitting bottom" and not enabling or rescuing those that will not or cannot yet help themselves to change. One such woman was asked to leave treatment after once again allowing her husband back in the home and violating a protective order. She did not see the harm she was bringing to herself and her son, who hated the fights and never felt safe. She would say with a grin, "I give it just as much as I take it!" The story that follows addresses this issue.

THE RESCUE

"Help! Help!" she cried, as the riptide pulled her further and further out to sea. She swam with all her might against the current, but it was to no avail. Her heart was beating rapidly, and the hot sun blinded her. She was tiring quickly and it seemed she would soon drown if no one heard her cries and came to save her.

The lifeguard on shore heard her cries and swam quickly out to where the woman was struggling. He put her in a hold and swam sideways, breathing heavily with exertion, towing her along, until both were outside the riptide's deathly grip. He started to swim toward shore with the woman now limp in his arms.

Suddenly, the lifeguard took a good look at the victim's face, stopped swimming, and dropped her into the water. He exclaimed, "What the hell?! It's you again!"

"Yah," said the swimmer, now standing up on her own. She grinned. "Thank you for saving me!"

The lifeguard was frowning. "I saved you three times last week—and again today. What is going on? If I didn't know better, I might think you swim in the riptide on purpose."

The woman had trouble looking him in the eye. "Well," she said, "I know I should stay out of the riptide, but the whole experience gives me a real adrenaline rush; so instead of moving sideways and escaping, I dive straight into it."

"Adrenaline rush?" he asked.

"Yes," she replied. "First I feel the strength of the tide—it overpowers me and I get a nearly orgasmic thrill at being so close to death; I figure you will save me so I don't really worry. And then afterward everyone on shore wants to make sure I'm OK. They ask me to tell my story; and I make a lot of new friends. Sometimes a cute guy even brings me a margarita or a piña colada while I'm recovering on the beach."

The lifeguard was dumfounded and didn't quite know what to say.

"You could drown!" he said. "There might come a time when I can't get to you in time. Or someone else might try to save you, and that person could drown. You are taking far too great a risk for a little attention and a piña colada."

"Well that's the way I am, take me or leave me," said the woman.

The lifeguard needed no further invitation. He decided to ban her from the beach from that day forward, because he needed to save his energy and rescue people that really needed it—people that *accidentally* got overpowered by the riptide and might drown without his help.

The lifeguard was wise enough to know that if the woman was going to put *herself* at risk over and over again, he could not rescue her or prevent her self-destruction. The lifeguard was wise enough to know the difference between what he could change and what he could not.

THE BOTTOM LINE: Stay out of the riptide!

FOOD FOR THOUGHT QUESTIONS

1. Give an example of a time you or someone else used drama to get attention.
2. Discuss a time you took an unnecessary risk.
3. Ask yourself, "How am I most like the woman in this story?"
4. What is your riptide?

6

Confronting Entitlement

The attitude of entitlement is rearing its ugly head when an angry partner says, "She deserved it" after shoving his wife down the stairs; or a mother says to the CPS investigator, "She had it coming" after popping her pre-teen daughter in the mouth for talking back. Until someone recognizes the need to change behavior, change must be imposed externally for the sake of safety, often through a DVO court order or CPS action.

Parents that use "blame" language teach their children to use "blame" language. They blame others when things go wrong and believe they are entitled to retaliation. Many families that live in violence abide by the "pay-back principle," which is one of revenge. They give back whatever they get; and the grudges they hold last a lifetime.

The problem with entitlement is that it makes the individual believe that he or she has the right to do whatever that person pleases—such as abuse in the name of "Discipline," rape in the name of "Married Sex," and Dis-honesty in the name of "What I Deserve."

It is likely during Pre-Contemplation that a person will need external safety parameters imposed by the court or an agency. But through account-ability and feedback, someone can consider his or her impact on others and move toward the next step of change.

POOP IN THE BARNYARD

It was a cloudy, rainy day in the barnyard, and the animals did not sound happy.

Samantha Sheep was baaing for her breakfast. Watch Dog was barking to play a game of fetch. Barn Cat was meowing for someone to pet her. Milk Cow was mooing for someone to milk her. Wagon Horse was snorting and stomping his hooves in the barnyard dirt waiting for someone to groom him. Usually by now the girl had come to take care of their needs.

The girl, Jenny, was sitting on the barnyard fence, smirking at the animals and swinging her feet, her hair and clothing soaking wet. "So there!" she said to the animals.

"What was going on?" you ask.

Well let me continue the story.

"Jenny," called out the little girl's mother from the front porch of the house. "Did you do your chores like I asked?"

Jenny hated rainy days. The dark, cloudy, rainy days on the farm made her sulk and pout. And when she pouted, she did not want to listen to her mother or to anyone else, for that matter. So, she sat on the fence and ignored her mother.

Jenny's mother had sent her daughter out to the barnyard to feed Samantha Sheep, play fetch with Watch Dog, pet Barn Cat, milk the Milk Cow, and groom Wagon Horse. She suspected that Jenny had not done her chores—usually after she did her chores, she came right back in the house, especially on a rainy day. She did not usually sit in the rain on the barnyard fence.

Jenny's mother grabbed an umbrella and headed toward the barnyard to talk to her daughter.

When Jenny saw her mother, she wiped the smirk off her face.

The mother could see that each animal had brown stuff on his or her face. She didn't know what it was, but she immediately suspected her daughter. "Tell me the truth Jenny," said her mother. "What have you done to the animals?"

Jenny said, in a very grouchy, sullen voice, "I was going into the barnyard to do my chores and I stepped in poop: sheep poop, cat poop, horse poop, and cow poop. The animals have pooped all over the barnyard and their poop has ruined my new tennis shoes!"

Her mother frowned. "Jenny, that's what animals do. And when they are upset for not being milked, or fed, or groomed, they poop even more. You know that. I can see that you didn't do your chores. But answer my earlier question. What have you done to the animals? There is brown stuff on their faces."

Jenny decided to avoid answering her mother's question—she was afraid she would get in trouble for what she had done. Jenny had been grouchy and pouty that morning and she had taken it out on the animals.

Jenny said, "Mom, I was in a bad mood when I woke up today, and there was just too much poop in the barnyard. It made my mood even worse. It smelled awful. It looked nasty. And there were flies all over it."

"Yes," said her mother, "poop smells. And it looks nasty. And flies get all over it. But what did you do to the animals?"

Jenny looked down and said, cautiously, "I gave it back to them—flung their poop in their faces. And I rubbed Barn Cat's face in it, too. They deserved it—it was their fault that my new tennis shoes are ruined!"

Jenny had been right that she would get in trouble. Her mother was very unhappy with Jenny's decision to fling animal poop back in the animals' faces.

"Jenny!" said her mother sternly. "I understand that you were in a bad mood. But it is not OK to take your mood out on poor, defenseless animals. They depend on you and me to take care of them. Flinging poop back in their faces only makes things worse."

Jenny's mom told her to clean up the rest of the poop in the barnyard with a shovel and to wash off the animals' faces with a hose. After that, she still had to do all her chores and would be grounded. Jenny didn't like it, but it didn't matter. Poop may be dark and nasty and smell bad, but everyone knows that poop is part of life on a farm. When you find poop in a barnyard, you clean it up—you never throw it in anyone's face!

You will be glad to hear that her mother made sure Jenny took better care of the animals from that day on. I wish I could tell you Jenny's mood improved right away, but it didn't. She was a rather self-centered, immature girl that needed to learn how to be kind to others, including animals, and that would take some time.

THE BOTTOM LINE: Flinging poop makes matters worse!

FOOD FOR THOUGHT QUESTIONS

1. Give an example of a time you "flung poop" in someone's face. How were you feeling? What did you do? How did that person respond?
2. What could you do to clean up your poop?
3. How do you feel when someone else flings poop in your face?

Part II

STORIES FOR CONTEMPLATION

The stories in this section seed the possibility of change by opening up awareness. They help a woman figure out where she is now and where she wants to be. Women in the Contemplation Stage are aware of problems in their relationships but not yet committed to making a significant life change. It is the stage in which stories will elicit thoughts and feelings about the risks and benefits of possible changes.

This stage can last a very long time (DiClemente & Velasquez, 2002). The woman is usually "on the fence" and spends more time thinking than doing. Often she thinks about all the reasons she would like to change but can't. She worries about how her children and family will react, or she fears retaliation from her partner. The first step toward change is often the hardest.

The therapist's role during this phase is to "sit on the fence" of the client's ambivalence with one leg on either side, never fully jumping off to one side or the other. When a therapist jumps to one side of the fence, sooner or later the client will jump to the other side and leaving the therapist dialectically behind. A clear example of this was the client who kept leaving her husband after he had an affair or lied to her. The therapist unwittingly supported her negative appraisal of the spouse, only to find them back together in a few weeks. The therapist needed to support the client, point out the ambivalence and follow her as she flip-flopped back and forth. One of the surest things to happen in therapy is that if the therapist tries to fix the client's situation or directly suggests how the client might change, then the client will come up with all the reasons why change is not possible at this point in time.

7

Peeling Away Defenses

Old habits die hard! Someone who has been using protective behaviors for years may not even remember where it all started. Therapeutic self-understanding is an "undressing" process, whereby a client takes off the layers of old habits, comfortable behaviors, and safe emotional responding to reveal his or her innermost self.

I keep a set of nesting wooden Russian dolls in my office, and many clients can't resist opening them one by one until they get to the little "baby" doll at the center. As clients open the dolls, it is easier to talk about their life experiences and the layers of the self. In therapy, as long as they have a safe, trusting therapeutic alliance, most women can get to the core of their earliest attachment experiences. They find the courage to face the losses and disappointments they experienced as children and grow stronger within.

Women may point out recent events in their lives as the "reason" they stay or leave relationships or why they use drugs or why they have emotional problems. They don't realize at first that early life events impact later functioning. Through treatment, women discover that anger is a surface emotion under which pain, grief, and fear reside.

One young mother blamed her partners and others for her angry outbursts, not connecting her mood-regulation problems to the early tragic loss of her mother and siblings and the subsequent abuse and neglect by her father. The story that follows invites women to "strip off" their protective defenses and explore what lies within.

POLLY'S PLIGHT

Someone was waiting on the sidewalk to cross the street. You will notice that I did not call the person "he" or "she." That is because you could not tell if it was a man or a woman. The person was covered from head to toe in a suit of armor, except for two dark eyes peering out of the opening over the face.

The light turned green, and the person stepped awkwardly off the curb, one stiff leg at a time. "Clunk, clunk, CLUNK!"

A little girl on the other side of the street tugged at her mother's sleeve. "Mom, look over there!" she cried out as she pointed to the armored person now sprawled on the pavement. "Let's go help!"

Her mother agreed, so they crossed the street after looking both ways for cars. The two of them approached the metal-covered person, who was clanking and rolling around, trying to get back up.

The girl looked down and said, "Can we help you up before a car hits you?"

"Thank you," said the person. "It's hard to move around in this armor, and I can't see where I am going."

So they each offered a hand and pulled the person to his or her feet. "Busses, and taxis, and cars, oh my!" exclaimed the girl in an excited, scared voice as the three of them walked arm in arm to the other side of the street.

"Just kidding," she said with a smile. "I always did like that scene from *The Wizard of Oz.*"

When they were nearly at the curb, the girl said, "Be careful now, and step up over the curb with your left foot."

"OK," said the person in armor, with a smile in his or her voice, as he or she stepped carefully up over the curb, one stiff leg at a time. "Clunk, clunk."

Once they were all up on the sidewalk, the girl asked, "What's your name?"

The person answered, "My name is Polly."

Then the little girl asked, "Isn't it awful warm in there?"

Polly replied, "Yes, but I'm used to it. I have worn this armor since I was a girl."

The girl asked some more questions. "Why do you wear it? What do you look like under the armor?"

The girl's mother stopped her. "Please leave Polly alone. You are asking too many questions."

Polly replied, again with a smile in her voice. "It's OK. I can answer your daughter's questions. I wear it for protection. I don't really know what I look like under the armor, since I've worn it for such a long time."

The little girl asked, "Protection from what?"

Polly replied, "I don't really know anymore. I used to need it. I guess I could take it off."

The girl said, "Let us help you. You'll be much more comfortable."

"OK," Polly agreed. So they all pulled and tugged on pieces of armor until a huge pile of metal was lying on the sidewalk.

"Oh my goodness!" exclaimed the girl as she stared at Polly in surprise. "Mom, look what Polly's wearing under the armor!"

Polly looked like a human cocoon, with layers and layers of fabric, tape, and other things wrapped around her. The outside layer, now that the armor was gone, was Velcro. It, of course, was very rough and prickly.

The girl said, "Polly, you are wearing Velcro and so many other layers under the armor. Why do you wear so many layers?"

Polly replied, "When I was about your age, something bad happened to me, and I wanted to cover up. The first layer was a furry coat—it made me feel safe at a bad time in my life. After that, whenever anything bad happened to me, I added a new layer." Polly added, "The layers protect me. If I fall down, I bounce back up. I can't scrape my elbows or knees. If someone hits me, I can't feel it."

The little girl then asked, "What other layers do you have?"

Polly replied, "Let me think a minute so I don't get them out of order . . ."

Then she began,

"Layer #1 is a furry coat.

"Layer #2 is a black leather jacket.

"Layer #3 is a "heavy-duty" tin foil mummy wrap.

"Layer #4 is duct tape.

"Layer #5 is a hand-stitched quilt.

"Layer #6 is a down jacket.

"Layer #7 is an insulated black diver's suit.

"Layer #8 is a lamb's wool cape.

"Layer #9 is a sandpaper poncho.

"I'm not sure about layers 10 and 11."

Polly added, "And as you can see, the top layer now, #12, is Velcro, prickly side out. Layer #13 was my suit of armor.

"You know," she said, "I added the armor when someone poked me with a barbeque skewer. I figured nothing could get through a suit of armor."

The girl commented, "I don't really see why you stay all covered up. You have protection from injury and pain—but you can't feel ANYTHING! You can't feel the sun on your skin or the rain on your face. If someone gave you a hug, you would never know it. And it must be very hard to ride a bicycle or walk up a hill."

Polly admitted, "It's true that I miss hugs, and I wish I could feel rain and sunshine on my face. But I'd rather be safe than sorry. My layers keep me safe."

The little girl asked, "How do you know you still need all those layers? Can't you take a few off? Just because you needed them before doesn't mean you need them now."

Polly wrinkled up her forehead and closed her eyes, thinking. Then, with her eyes wide open, she said, "Well I guess I could take off the Velcro and a few other layers. I might be able to move around better."

The girl and her mother said, "We can help." Polly lifted her arms up over her head, and they helped her take off the Velcro. As the last strip of Velcro came off, they saw layer #11, a layer of soft red flannel, underneath.

"This is a real adventure," said Polly. "I forgot there was a soft flannel layer underneath the rough Velcro. Let's see what's next!"

Together they peeled off the flannel and then layer #10, which turned out to be clingy cellophane. When they got down to layer #9, the sandpaper poncho, Polly said goodbye to the girl and her mother.

"That's enough for one day," she announced. "I need to think about how many more layers to take off. Let's meet again tomorrow—3 o'clock at Pernicano's Pizza." The girl and her mother agreed and went on their way.

Their waitress came to the table and looked at Polly very strangely, probably because Polly was wearing the sandpaper poncho.

"A large double cheese, double pepperoni and a pitcher of root beer," they said.

And then, while they waited for their pizza, the girl and her mother helped Polly peel off the rest of the layers, one by one. Polly kept exclaiming things like, "Ooh, that one's ugly!" or "Duct tape is so hard to take off in a restaurant!"

Layer by layer came off. Polly began to look less round and a little more human. Soon they could see a sweet smile, rosy cheeks, and dark eyes.

"You're very attractive," said the girl. "But you hid it well."

"That's OK," said Polly, "Until now it didn't matter."

At the furry coat, the last layer, Polly paused for a long time. She looked serious and sad. "I don't know if I can take this one off. It brings back bad memories."

The girl replied, "It's OK—you don't need it anymore. You don't need to hide *any* part of you."

Polly realized that the bad times had not changed *who* she was—they had changed how she saw herself.

And so Polly unbuttoned the furry coat, took it off, and dropped it to the ground. "Now I can finally see who you really are," said the little girl.

Just then, the waitress brought their large triple pepperoni, double cheese pizza to the table. She put it down and sliced it with a metal wheel. "There's something different about you," she said to Polly as she tried to figure out what had changed.

"I can't figure it out," she said, "but whatever it is, it is a good change!" Polly and the girl shared a smile, because they agreed with the waitress. It was a very good change, indeed.

THE BOTTOM LINE: Peel it off—one layer at a time!

FOOD FOR THOUGHT QUESTIONS

1. How are you like Polly?
2. What are some of your layers?
3. What would it take for you to take off your layers? Can you do it alone or do you need help?
4. When do you feel most threatened or vulnerable and need to cover up?
5. What would be the hardest layer for you to take off?

8

Safety for Self and Others

Too often abuse victims grow up, select unfit partners, have children, and then expose their children to danger by living with those abusive partners and engaging in risky lifestyles. They also have unreasonable expectations for their children. I once had a very self-absorbed client who answered "no" to the question "Have you ever abused your children?"

As it turned out, she had exposed her children to a number of risks, directly and indirectly. She left them once overnight with a *new friend* who offered to babysit, then did not think she was responsible when that person called CPS due to her not coming back when planned. She allowed her third husband to lock them in a dark attic without food or light overnight, for their own good as a disciplinary technique, but she provided them with blankets so they would not get cold. She pointed out that she "protected" her children by sending them to another room or asking them to run next door when her husband was choking her. She allowed her four- and six-year-olds to go down the block to "play with" an older man that liked "hosting" neighborhood girls, in spite of signs that the older girl was becoming sexually reactive and aggressive toward others.

What she did not understand was that repeated exposure to maltreatment, direct or indirect, leaves children feeling very unsettled. The loud, angry, threatening voices they hear behind closed doors terrify them. Children move into pseudo-maturity, freeze, fight, or flee in the face of real or perceived danger; and these coping responses will continue unless they are given a true safety net from violence. The following story was written for a mom who did not realize the risks of exposing her children to abusive partners and a chaotic, volatile lifestyle. Whatever choices women make for themselves, they need to be aware of their children's needs for safety and "do the right thing."

THE BALANCING ACT

"Oh my gosh!" gasped the crowd as the pink flamingo danced across the tightrope, one leap at a time. "She's on the high wire without a safety net!"

It was true. There was no net to catch Fannie if she fell.

"Oops!" went Fannie, at least every other leap as she slipped on the wire and nearly fell to her death. She finally made it to the platform on the other side—wobbling, swaying, and slipping all the way.

It was the opening night of the circus, supposedly a family-friendly event.

"What if she falls? Why isn't she using a net?" asked the worried parents and children.

Over and over the circus manager had asked Fannie to use a safety net, but Fannie Flamingo refused.

"I like the excitement," said Fannie. "I like the feeling of total freedom. After all, what good is life if you can't take a little risk, face a little danger?"

"But you need to be safe—especially with children watching you," replied the circus manager.

"They can take me or leave me," answered Fannie with a big smile. "If they want to be entertained, they've come to the right place; and dancing on the high wire gives me a real thrill. They're a bunch of wimps if they can't stop worrying about me falling."

"But Fannie," said the manager. "The next time you fall, it will surely be to your death."

As you might have guessed, Fannie had fallen from the high wire before—twice to be exact. Both times, the magician and his crew had been able to get a trampoline under her before she hit the ground.

"I'm willing to take that chance," said Fannie.

"Well, I'm not willing to take the chance of you falling to your death in front of a bunch of children!" said the manager. "Next time you do your act, use the safety net!"

The following night of the circus, it came time for Fannie's big act, and out she came, tall and pink in a sparkly costume.

"Oh look!" the crowd cried out. "What cute little flamingo babies."

It was true. Fannie had brought her two flamingo babies with her to watch her act.

"Sit here and watch your mommy," she said as she led them to the front row of seats. "See how brave I am? Mommy isn't afraid of anything!"

"But we are, Mommy," said her oldest child. "Where is the safety net? You know the manager told you to use it."

"Pish-posh!" said Fannie. "I'm feeling lucky tonight. I'll be fine, with or without a safety net. And I feel more creative and artistic without it."

"Don't cry!" she said as she saw the tears in her children's eyes.

As her babies and everyone else watched, Fannie climbed the tall ladder, stepped out on the tightrope, and began to dance across.

Slip! "Gasp!" Slip! "Gasp!"

"Please stop, Mommy!" The small, tearful voice came from the front row.

Fannie ignored her child and leaped across the wire. As she approached the platform on the other side, she started to wobble, first right, then left. Swan grabbed her and pulled her to safety.

The crowd gasped in relief.

Fannie took a bow, then climbed down the ladder and went over to where her children were sitting. She put a baby flamingo on each shoulder, and headed back toward the ladder.

"What is she doing?" murmured the crowd. "Surely she won't take them up on that high wire without a safety net!"

Fannie grabbed the microphone and announced, "Yes, it's what you've all been waiting for—The Family Flamingo Act! A death-defying feat with no safety net! You won't believe your eyes!"

She slowly climbed the tall ladder with two frightened babies on her shoulders. They clung to her feathers and hid their heads.

"Don't worry," Fannie whispered to her children. "Mommy promises that the magician will bring out the trampoline if we fall."

"But Mommy," whimpered the babies. "We don't *want* to fall. And we don't like heights. Please don't take us out on the high wire."

"Don't be such cry babies!" said Fannie. "You're old enough to have a little fun and excitement."

Fannie didn't realize that what was fun and exciting for her was terrifying for her children. She had gotten too caught up in her free-spirited life and forgotten what was best for her babies.

As she reached the top of the ladder and stood on the platform, Fannie found Swan blocking her way to the wire.

"Get out of my way!" said Fannie.

"No," said the swan. "I can't let you do this. The risks are too great. You have to make a choice. You can exercise your right to freedom and choose to self-destruct, but you can't take your children with you."

Fannie wasn't really a *bad* mother—just uninformed. She had simply forgotten that adults must protect children from things that could hurt them. Sometimes you have to change your lifestyle a bit for the sake of your children.

Fannie grumbled and groaned, but she realized that Swan was right. She climbed down the ladder and put her children back in their front-row seats.

"You can just watch," said Fannie to her children. "Sorry I put you through all that . . ."

Then Fannie summoned the manager. "OK," she said, "I get it. I need to use the safety net for the sake of the children."

She added, "You understand that if it was just me, I would continue my act without it."

"Whatever you say, Fannie," said the manager. "But I'm glad you came to your senses. You were scaring everyone—maybe more than you realized. When your babies are older, perhaps they will join you on the high wire, but certainly not without a safety net. After all, it is better to be safe than sorry."

THE BOTTOM LINE: It *is* better to be safe than sorry!

FOOD FOR THOUGHT QUESTIONS

1. Give an example of a time you set a bad example for someone else.
2. Describe a time when your behavior (mood, words, actions) scared someone else.
3. What is your safety net?
4. Do you ever do risky things without a safety net? Please discuss.

9

The Blame Game

The woman had been told since she was little, first by her mother, then her stepfather, next by her boyfriend, and later by her husband, "You are bad—what happened is all your fault." When she was five and her two-year-old sister left the house and wandered into the street while the mother slept, the woman had been blamed. "It's your fault someone called CPS. You should have woken me up. You know she's not allowed in the street." When her mother and stepfather split up after two years, he told her, "It's your fault—all we do is fight about you!" When her 20-year-old boyfriend got her drunk at age 14 and then raped her, he said, "You know you wanted it. You could hardly keep your hands off me last night." And five years later, when her drunken husband broke her nose during a domestic dispute, her neighbors called the police and the police arrested him. She said, "I shouldn't have yelled at him for spending the rent money on drugs. It's my fault he hit me."

This woman had to change her perception in order to stop blaming herself for things that were not her fault. Beliefs and attitudes start to form at an early age, and children internalize what they are told. Ultimately, many young, egocentric children assume they are the cause of the bad things in their lives.

The story that follows is dedicated to an 11-year-old girl whose mother shaved her head as punishment for not taking care of her thick, unruly hair. Her mother could not recognize that this behavior had been abusive. It is important that abuse victims receive support from those outside their families and be exposed to views that challenge what they have been taught.

WHOSE FAULT IS IT ANYWAY?

Ever since she was born, seven-year-old Gloria Gorilla had heard, "It's all your fault." When the bananas for breakfast got overripe, her mother said, "It's all your fault!" If her mother had a bad day she shrieked, as apes do, "Ah-ah-ah-ah-ah, Gloria, it's all your fault." When Gloria's dad left her mother for a younger gorilla, once again her mother said, "It's all your fault!"

It wasn't true, you know. None of those things were Gloria's fault. But Gloria believed what her mother told her, as young gorillas most often do. Now, Gloria's mother's voice lived inside her daughter's head. Whenever something bad happened, the voice said, "Gloria, it's all your fault!"

One day, the clouds came out when they were having a picnic. The wind blew and the rain started to fall. "It's all my fault," said Gloria. That is very silly, you know, because children can't make it rain.

Another day, her mother screamed and shouted at Gloria's dad on the phone. As Gloria listened to the phone call, she thought, "It's all my fault." It was not true. Her mother was upset about Gloria's dad leaving her.

Gloria blamed herself for almost everything. If a chair fell on her foot, she said, "I'm so clumsy." When her mother overslept and Gloria missed the school bus, Gloria said, "I'm sorry Mom. I should have waked you up." When her father cancelled their visit for a business meeting, Gloria said, "My dad doesn't want to see me. I must have done something to upset him." And as you know, none of these things were Gloria's fault. But sometimes the blaming voice in your head talks louder than your common sense. After awhile, you can't tell what is true.

Gloria's mother was very unhappy; and more and more, she took it out on Gloria. She had always had mood swings, but it had gotten worse since Gloria's dad left. Then, one morning, which turned out to be a very bad morning, Gloria's mother yelled, "Gloria, come here, I want to brush your hair."

Gloria had beautiful, long, thick black hair, but she was too young to take care of it by herself. Her mother usually helped her brush it and sometimes even put ribbons in it. When her mother brushed it every day, it stayed shiny and untangled. But lately, her mother had forgotten to brush her daughter's hair.

"I hate it when my mom wakes up in a bad mood," thought Gloria. "But I'm glad she offered to brush my hair!"

Gloria walked over to her mother, who sat down behind her and pulled the brush harshly through the small gorilla's hair.

"What a tangled mess!" exclaimed Gloria's mother.

Tears came to Gloria's eyes. "Owww," she cried. "That hurts." The brush had caught in a tangle. Gloria flinched and pulled away, which hurt even more.

"Don't get started!" ordered Gloria's mother. "It's your own fault that it hurts. You let your hair get all tangled. Now hold still while I brush it. You're too big to be such a crybaby."

Gloria thought, "It's all my fault. I let my hair get tangled."

Well, everyone knows that little gorillas need help taking care of their thick hair.

Her mother brushed harder and harder. Clumps of hair came out. Gloria kept pulling away and crying. I'm sure you understand why. It hurts a lot to have your mother pull your hair out.

Her mother became more and more angry because the brush would not go through the thick hair.

"That's it! I've had enough!" said her mother, who went into the bathroom and came out with the scissors and dog clippers. Before Gloria could say a word, her mother cut off her beautiful thick hair and shaved Gloria's head bald.

"There," she said, "a perfect solution—one I hope you'll remember. You deserved to be punished for not taking care of your hair. It's all your fault."

Shaving Gloria's head was not a perfect or even good solution. Many people would have called it gorilla abuse. Gloria sobbed all the way to gorilla school that day, swinging from vine to vine. When she arrived at school, some of the other children made fun of her bald head and others hung back in shocked silence.

"It's all my fault," sobbed Gloria.

Gloria's teacher, a kind swan, was greeting students at the school door. She was shocked at the sight of Gloria's head and tears came to her eyes. She had never seen a small gorilla with a shaved head. How could anyone do such a thing?!

The teacher said, "Gloria, come with me," and took Gloria to a little bench under a tree where they could talk privately. The teacher put her wing around Gloria and offered her a banana. Gloria leaned her head against the teacher's feathered breast.

"Gloria," said the teacher in a concerned voice. "Tell me what happened to your hair."

"Why is my teacher being so nice?" thought Gloria. "It's all my fault." But Gloria trusted her teacher, so she told her about the haircut and other things that had been happening at home.

"Gloria," said her teacher, "those things that happened at home were not your fault. Your mother seems to be having a hard time since your father left, but it was wrong for her to shave your head. Now wait here for a minute and I'll be right back."

The teacher went into the school and came out a few minutes later with a pretty scarf to wrap around Gloria's bald head.

"Thank you for the scarf," said Gloria shyly.

Her teacher said, "Gloria, grownups have problems that children can't understand. You need to stop blaming yourself for your parents' problems and for things that are outside your control."

Gloria replied, "But I have my mother's voice inside my head. It tells me that everything is my fault."

The teacher suggested, "You need a new voice in your head—a friendly voice.

"Hmmm," said Gloria. "I could use a friendly voice in my head—one that doesn't sound like my mother's. What would a friendly voice say?" she asked her teacher.

"Oh, you know," said her teacher. "Things like, 'It's not your fault. You don't need to be perfect. It's OK to make mistakes. You are good just the way you are.' Maybe that would help."

For the rest of the day Gloria wore the scarf and imagined a friendly voice in her head, one that blocked out her mother's voice—in her mind, the voice sounded a little like her teacher's. She had trouble believing the kind words, but it was a nice change.

"Hang in there," it said. "What's going on at home is not your fault. You are OK just the way you are!"

At the end of the school day, Gloria's teacher pulled her aside once more.

"Gloria," she said, "I called your dad, and he'll pick you and your brothers and sisters up from school today. We're going to get your mother some help for her problems."

Gloria loved her dad and thought it would be OK to live with him and his girlfriend while her mother worked on her problems. He worked at the banana factory and was a fun-loving ape that liked to swing from vines and climb trees. He never told Gloria that things were all her fault.

Gloria listened to the kind *teacher voice* in her head, and the funny thing was that Gloria started to *believe* the nice things her new voice said about her.

One Saturday while the family was eating lunch, her dad said, "We're going to take you all to the park later this afternoon." Gloria didn't want to go to the park because she was reading a good book about vampires and wished it would rain. About an hour later, it started to rain.

Guess what Gloria did? Gloria thought, "IT'S NOT MY FAULT! I sure don't have the power to make it rain!"

You can see how far she had come. Gloria had figured out that wishing for something is not the same thing as making it happen.

She could not resist a small smile, though. "It is nice," she thought, "when things *happen* to go my way!"

THE BOTTOM LINE: Sometimes STUFF Just Happens!

FOOD FOR THOUGHT QUESTIONS

1. How are you like Gloria
2. How are you like Gloria's mother?
3. What things do you blame yourself for the most?
4. Do you blame yourself for things that aren't your fault? Give an example.

10

Self-Protection

Abused and neglected children often have fathers who are absent, "mood-altered," mean, or dismissive toward women. Some learned from their experiences that a man was free to spend his money and time as he wished, with little or no accountability. They came to believe that a man can do as he pleases and that no one should tell him what to do.

Women who have been victims of domestic violence may have dysfunctional attitudes about sex and may not know how to set limits with their partners. They let them return for "makeup sex" or a place to sleep in spite of protective orders.

In a women's group I was leading, the participants talked openly about their sexual experiences. One admitted, "I got pregnant with my daughter when I was 14. No one talked to me about any of that. I had to do what he wanted or he would leave." She moved from childhood straight into parenthood before she was ready. Another woman saw sex as a handy way of controlling men; she had worked as a stripper and pole/lap dancer and liked being in charge at the club. There, she could "call the shots."

Several women in the group talked about engaging in unprotected sex. They knew the risks but didn't feel they could object or insist that the man wear a condom. "He says it don't feel good to wear a rubber," said a mother who had six children by age 25. "I ain't going to tell him he has to wear a rubber because then I won't get any, and I like sex." Nearly all the women in the group knew the risk of unprotected sex (HIV and other STDs), yet they did not know how to say no.

Following are some statements about sexual behavior that the group eventually came up with. It is certainly not where they started, but it was a good place to be in the end:

- It is better to take care of your sexual needs yourself (or be celibate) than to have unprotected sex.
- Tell your partner what you like in sex.
- Say no to sexual requests that are risky or make you feel bad.
- Sometimes he is "in it" for himself and doesn't care about your needs or the risks.
- You need to know the difference between sex and love.
- No force or threats in sex—that is a form of rape or abuse—"no" means "no."
- Set good boundaries (don't sleep with everyone)—you set the example for your kids.
- He should treat you kindly and with respect.
- Don't use sex to get high or avoid feelings.
- You don't have to share him/her with others.

The following story portrays the risks of going along with the high-risk suggestions of a man that has only his own interests in mind.

KEEP THE SAFETY ON THE GUN

Heather Hen and Suzie Swan entered Carl's Casino on the Strip and Heather exclaimed, "I've never been anywhere so fancy! Look, Suzie, see all the flashing lights and hear all the slot machines ringing. I hardly know where to start!"

Heather and Suzie had ridden the farm wagon into town for the day. Neither had ever been very far from home; and the glitter of the casino was so different from the dusty barnyard. They stared at all the interesting looking people and heard coins clattering into bins as people hit jackpots.

"I see a bingo hall over there," said Suzie. "I know how to play it, and I won't lose a lot of money."

"I want something more exciting," declared Heather. "I think I'll try my hand at a slot machine or blackjack."

The friends parted and agreed to meet later for lunch.

Heather turned her $20 bill into coins and sat down at a nickel slot. The money went fast, but every so often Heather would match two cherries or three dollar signs, and coins would clatter into her bin. She could not resist continuing, and her pile of nickels grew smaller and smaller.

"Just a couple more," she thought. "This machine hasn't paid off in awhile. It's due to pay off soon."

As she lost her last nickel, she heard a deep voice behind her. "Hi honey. What brings a cute chick like you to Carl's? I haven't seen you here before."

She looked around. There was a cocky, handsome, bold rooster. Was he talking to her? "Oh my," thought Heather. "That handsome rooster is flirting with ME!"

The first thing she could think to say was, "My friend and I came to check out the new casino. We live on a farm ten miles out of town."

The rooster announced, "My name's Randy Rooster. Why don't we hang out and I'll show you the ropes." At that moment the waitress came to take drink orders and Randy smoothly ordered two drinks. "It's on me," he told Heather.

Randy suggested they go play blackjack.

"I'm out of money," said Heather.

"It's OK, honey, it's on me," Randy replied.

Heather didn't know how to play, but Randy quickly taught her the game, and they played at a busy table.

Randy talked a lot about himself and bragged about what a great gambler he was. He didn't ask Heather any questions about herself but kept ordering drinks and betting large sums of money. He was dressed really flashy in nice clothes, and he had a smooth, polished look to him.

"I'm a little out of my league," thought Heather, but she was flattered by the attention and after a few drinks she felt her guard coming down.

Before long, Randy was hitting on her. He put his wing around her and squeezed her in places she had not been squeezed in a long time. What a horny rooster! Or maybe it was the alcohol. . . . And every time Randy won a blackjack hand, he got flushed and more excited.

Randy abruptly announced, "Enough of this blackjack, honey. I get bored easily. I need a little more excitement. Let's go to the craps table."

Heather followed Randy to the craps table and sat down next to him. He tried to explain the game, but it was a lot more complicated than blackjack. And there was more risk, since it was hard to win against the house. Heather decided just to watch.

In a very short time, all of Randy's money was gone. Randy asked her to use her credit card to get more cash from the ATM. Heather figured she could make it up in her next paycheck and withdrew $100. She was enjoying Randy's attention, and she didn't want to tell him no.

Heather returned to the craps table, but once again, Randy abruptly suggested they move on. "Honey let's go in the back room now and play a high-risk game. It's one that gets me really excited. I only take special chicks to the back room."

Heather felt a moment of alarm (she didn't know Randy very well) but didn't say anything, and she followed Randy to the back room. After all, it was a casino. What could possibly go wrong?

The back room was dark, filled with small tables and couples in various states of undress.

Heather sat down next to Randy at a table, and he said, "No honey, sit in my lap. It makes me feel really good when a beautiful chick sits in my lap."

So Heather sat in Randy's lap. As her eyes adjusted to the darkness, she saw two people at the next table. One person held a gun to the other person's head and pulled the trigger. Heather jumped as the gun clicked, but nothing happened. The people both laughed and took a drink. Then one of them took off an item of clothing.

Heather's heart jumped. "What are they doing?" she asked.

Randy said, "They're playing a game called strip roulette, only it's pretty tame, because the guns are only loaded with paint balls. Let's you and I play a more exciting game, one that's a REAL turn-on."

"What game is that?" asked Heather.

Randy picked up a gun off their table and said, "It's called 'The Real Thing'. I'll go first."

Before Heather could say a word, Randy took a bullet out of his coat pocket and loaded the gun. He spun the chambers and took off the safety. He smiled a sexy smile and said, "Are you ready?"

"Randy," said Heather, who started to get up from the table, "I don't want to play with a loaded gun. And I don't want to play with the safety off. Let's just play with the paint balls."

"Don't be a chicken," said Randy in a not-so-nice voice. "I treated you real nice and bought you drinks. Now you need to play my game."

"Randy," replied Heather, "I'm not like you and I don't like your game."

Randy kissed Heather and made her heart flutter. He crooned, "We've been having fun, right? I bet no one has kissed that pretty beak in a very long time. What good is living life if you don't live a little dangerously? You need to loosen up."

Randy added, "I like having the safety off when I fool around with a sexy chick. Keeping the safety on just doesn't do it for me. Using real bullets turns me on. There's nothing worse than shooting blanks."

Randy added, "You know, honey, there's only one bullet in the gun, and you'll probably get lucky."

He thought, "If I shoot her I can find some other cute chick to play with the next time I come here."

Heather almost said, "OK," but she heard a loud voice. It was Suzie.

"Heather, what are you doing in here? Someone in the bingo game warned me to stay out of this room and to stay away from Randy Rooster. He's dangerous. They say he plays high-risk games with chicks."

"Meddling bitch!" said Randy. "I would have scored with your clucking friend here if you had given us just a little more time."

Needless to say, Heather came quickly back to her senses and left with Suzie. She sobered up on the wagon ride back to the farm.

"Thanks, Suzie," said Heather. "I don't know what got into me. All that glitzy seduction got me carried away."

Suzie warned, "A little fun is fine, but never play games with Randy Rooster at Carl's Casino. Randy always wins, at the chick's expense."

Heather realized she had a lot to learn about men, gaming, and risk. One thing she knew for sure—a guy who asks you to play with an unlocked, loaded gun in a back room at a casino is *not in it for you*, and if you play along, the odds are all in his favor.

THE BOTTOM LINE: Play it safe with sex!

FOOD FOR THOUGHT QUESTIONS

1. How are you like Heather?
2. How are you like Suzie?
3. Describe one or more times you took a risk with a dangerous man.
4. How do you know when to say, "No"?

11

Warning Signs in Relationships

Women in domestically violent relationships do not accurately evaluate the qualities of their friends and partners. Some jump quickly into new relationships in spite of warning signs, and later they find themselves involved with potentially dangerous partners.

"He wasn't like that when I met him," said one client, after meeting a new man, giving him her address, introducing him to her children, and being assaulted in her apartment (in front of her children) two weeks after she broke up with him. He had come seeking drugs. "I broke up with him once he started acting controlling. It wasn't my fault it happened."

There had been some *warning signs* early on. But the client was so used to a "certain type" of man that she missed the cues. She rushed into intimacy so quickly that by the time she noticed warning signs it was too late.

The story that follows, *No More Rotten Eggs*, is about paying attention to things about a potential partner *before* entering into a relationship.

NO MORE ROTTEN EGGS

Carla Chicken's mother called out, banging on Carla's bedroom door. "Carla! Carla!"

"What, Mom?" Carla answered. It was noon on a cold Saturday morning. Carla was getting ready to take her shower, and her headphones, now hanging around her neck, were blaring out music from her IPod.

"I need to talk to you," said her Mom. "May I come in?"

"Oh-oh," thought Carla. "Here we go again! What have I done now? Did I sleep too late? Did I forget to put my dishes in the sink? Did I wake up Dad when I came in at 2 a.m.?"

Carla hated living at home. She had dropped out of school and could not yet afford to live on her own. It seemed like her mother was always getting into her business.

"Come in," said Carla.

Carla's mother came into the bedroom and wrinkled up her nose.

"What is that smell?" she asked.

"What smell," asked Carla.

"That rotten egg smell, so nasty it makes me want to puke," said her mother with a trace of sarcasm in her voice.

"Oh," said Carla, "*that* smell! Well, that smell probably came from Eddie Egg."

Carla was dating Eddie Egg, the twelfth egg Carla had dated in the last year—an even dozen.

She had dated Humpty Dumpty Egg before Eddie, but he had fallen off a wall two weeks ago. All the king's horses and men could not put him together again, so Carla had moved on.

You might remember the nursery rhyme about Humpty Dumpty. Let me clue you in on something the nursery rhyme didn't tell you. When Humpty Dumpty fell off the wall and broke into pieces, he smelled awful. He was rotten inside—on the outside he was so cute in his little shirt and tie, but on the inside, he was just one more smelly, rotten egg.

"Who is Eddie Egg?" asked Carla's mother.

"He's the guy I'm dating, Mom. You know, ever since Humpty Dumpty fell off the wall."

Carla's mother was not pleased. You see, she had known that Humpty was rotten inside. She had noticed the hairline crack on his underside and had tried to tell Carla, but her daughter wouldn't listen to her.

And she had tried to tell Carla about the ten eggs before him—they had been cracked and rotten as well. She knew that Carla was a grownup now and she should stay out of her business, but her daughter had terrible taste in eggs.

Her mother had told Carla, "You bring home too many rotten eggs. Everyone knows you need to check the eggs in the carton before you bring one home. It's easy for an egg to get cracked after it leaves the nest."

"Leave me alone, Mom," said Carla. "Who I date is my business!"

"Carla," said her mother, "I worry about you and wish you would be more careful. An egg might look OK at first glance, but you have to look for cracks. A nice, farm-fresh egg has no cracks and it doesn't smell. A smelly egg is rotten inside."

"Mom," said Carla, "Eddie is not cracked or rotten. He came here right from work and didn't have time to clean up. He usually smells fine."

"Carla," said her mother, "If you check Eddie out, I bet you'll find a crack."

"Not Eddie," said Carla. "I dated some rotten eggs before, but now I know what to look for." She sighed. "Once you get close to someone, it's harder to see the cracks. I had high hopes for me and Humpty Dumpty before he fell off the wall . . ."

Carla added, "But Eddie is not like the ten eggs before him. There's no way Eddie is cracked. He's very sweet. He dresses really sharp, takes me to the clubs, and has good taste in music."

"Oh Carla," said her mother, "it's easy for an egg to hide his cracks in the dark lights at the clubs. And anyone can sweet-talk a beautiful girl like you. Bad eggs try to make you think they are nicer than they really are."

"I know, Mom," replied Carla with a grin as she gave her mother a hug. "It's nice that you worry about me and don't want me to get hurt. But I'm a big girl now."

"Well," said her mother, "I just don't want to have to say, 'I told you so.'"

After her mom left the room, Carla went and took her shower, got dressed, and called Eddie on her cell phone. She agreed to go with Eddie to the club again that night.

Carla wasn't a total idiot. So later that night, before they went to the club, Carla invited Eddie over to meet her mother. She knew that she picked a lot of rotten eggs. And she wanted to prove her mother wrong.

"Why do you want me to meet your mother?" asked Eddie. He did not look very happy.

"We've been dating a couple of weeks now, and my mom wants to meet you," said Carla. She didn't want to tell Eddie it was *her* idea.

Eddie arrived at 9 p.m. and rang the doorbell of Carla's house. She answered the door as she called out, "Mom, Eddie is here. Come meet him so we can leave for the club."

"I wonder what's going on," thought Carla's mother. "Carla never wants me to meet her dates."

Carla turned on the bright lights of the front hallway and invited Eddie inside.

Eddie stepped inside and Carla sent her mother a look that said, "Get as close as you can and see if you can find a crack in this fine young egg."

Carla's mother stepped up close to Eddie to introduce herself.

"Hello Eddie. I'm Carla's mother. How are you?"

Eddie did not answer. He grunted, looked at the floor, and said, "Come on Carla. Let's go to the club."

As Eddie turned around to go back out the door, Carla's mother sniffed the air and looked pointedly at her daughter. Then Carla sniffed the air. She caught a whiff of something rotten.

Carla's mother pointed down at Eddie's bottom half and said, "Carla, isn't that a crack in Eddie's bottom half?"

"Why yes, Mom. I see what you mean," said Carla. She crossed her arms and looked Eddie straight in the eye. "Eddie," said Carla. "Are you a rotten egg?"

Eddie's face suddenly grew mean. "What's it to you?" he snarled. "Nosy B!" he added. "Sorry Carla, no club for me tonight."

Eddie strutted out the door and closed it in Carla's face.

Carla knew eggs-actly what her mother was thinking. "You were right, Mom," she said. "But better to find out now than later . . ."

Since Carla had now picked a dozen bad eggs, she decided to take a class called, Picking Out Good Eggs. During the weeks ahead, Carla learned lots of helpful hints. Things like, *Before you date an egg, look it over in bright light*; *Take an egg home to meet your family*; *Don't date an egg who uses air freshener every five minutes*; *Pick an egg that likes to talk with you*; and *Look for an egg who has left the nest.*"

Carla was hired soon after that as a *Courier Journal* features writer, and her column was "Carla's Guide for Picking a Good Egg"—she hoped that others might learn from her experiences. As everyone knows, rotten eggs are worth a dime a dozen, and Carla had learned she was worth a lot more than that!

THE BOTTOM LINE: No more rotten eggs!

FOOD FOR THOUGHT QUESTIONS

1. How are you like Carla?
2. Describe a few of your rotten eggs and how you got fooled.
3. Is it easy or hard for you to take advice from others about your relationships?

CARLA'S RULES FOR DATING

1. Consider abstaining from eggs while you are in early *relational recovery*.
2. Don't give out your address or bring him home until you know he is a "good egg."
3. Don't have your kids around him until you're ready for an exclusive relationship (so they don't get their hopes up and get hurt).
4. Meet him in public (at a safe place) until you know him better.
5. Wait to have sex—see if he hangs around without it. When you decide to have sex, use protection, and carry a condom in case he doesn't. Insist he wear it.
6. A good egg ADDS to your life and makes it better.
7. Good eggs bring out the best in one another.
8. A bad egg acts sorry and promises to change after he has been mean, controlling, or abusive, but it doesn't make up for how he treated you. It WILL happen again and it will get worse.
9. LOVE is not enough. It only takes one bad egg to ruin an omelet.
10. If he turns out to be a *bad* egg, leave and don't look back—you deserve better!

CARLA'S GUIDE FOR PICKING A GOOD EGG

- *Family*: Has he left the nest? How does he treat his family? Does he want me to meet his family and friends? Does he ask about my children or my family? Does he want to meet my friends?
- *Employment*: Does he have a job? How many jobs has he had? How long does he keep them?
- *Education*: Did he finish his education or is he working on it?
- *Lifestyle and Values*: Does he drink or do drugs? Does he sell drugs? Does he have a legal record? Is he honest with me? Did he cheat in a past relationship? (If yes, he may cheat again on me.) Does he run out of money and ask to borrow from me? Does he encourage me to make friends and spend time with them?
- *Attitude*: Does he blame other people for his problems? Is it always "hard luck" or "not fair"? Does he think he's always right? Does he make a lot of excuses? Can he say, "I'm sorry"? Does he keep score about money and who does what? Is he kind and generous? Is he controlling? Is he judgmental?
- *Interest in Partner*: Does he like to spend time with me? Does he ask what I want to do? Does he give me equal time with his friends? Does he usually come to me only for sex? Does he ask about my feelings?

Does he like to talk to me? Does he talk only about himself or does he show interest in me?

- *Trust:* Does he trust me? Is he suspicious? Does he try to control or check up on me, even in a "friendly" way? Does he ever, even once, check the mileage on my car?
- *Emotional:* Does he have a mean streak? Does he have a good sense of humor? Does he share his feelings? Does he have mood swings? Does he blame me for his moods? Has he ever shoved me when he's angry? Does he mistreat children? Does he avoid conflict (walk away, refuse to talk, give me the silent treatment).

12

Relationship Roles

Relationship roles are not "one type fits all"—they must be a *good fit* for an individual and his or her life circumstances. Some parents enjoy work outside the home and find their talents put to good use. Others prefer to stay home with their children. There are also women who would like to go to school or work outside the home, but they are constrained by doubt or by traditional or cultural belief systems. A woman's role should not be determined by the controlling or judgmental behaviors of others.

I have heard women say, "I'm too old to go back to school" or "I always dreamed of doing that but it'll never happen." A wise therapist once said, "You can do this thing, be old, and celebrate doing it before you die or you stay where you are, do nothing, and still be old and die, with nothing to celebrate."

Many victims of domestic violence are homeless, unemployed, under-educated, uninsured, or incarcerated. Higher level needs can't reasonably be pursued until lower survival needs such as food and shelter are met. A woman becomes free to realize talents and pursue her dreams once her basic needs are met. The story that follows, *The Rebellious Genie*, is a provocative commentary on traditional, hierarchical male-female relationships. Women need to be encouraged to follow their dreams.

THE REBELLIOUS GENIE

"Yes, Master," said the beautiful Jeanie Genie with a tantalizing smile as she came out of her bottle, ready to obey her master's request. Her lovely blond hair, colorful silk robes, and blousy pantaloons were a sight to behold.

"Your wish is my command. It is my duty to bring you pleasure and make you happy!"

I don't know about you, but hearing Jeanie talk like this makes me want to put a cork in her bottle! But she knew no other life. For the past 100 years, Jeanie had provided faithful service to the masters of her bottle. The routine had never changed—her master rubbed the bottle, called her name, and out she came to serve.

Jeanie's master had few demands. He summoned her to talk when he was lonely, or to cook and serve a sumptuous meal. At times he wanted her to join him in public so he could show her off to his friends; and on special occasions he asked her to perform personal favors. She was born to serve, or at least that's how she had been raised.

Today was Jeanie's birthday and her day off, so her genie friend Delilah had invited her out to lunch.

"Master," she said, "as you may remember, I'm spending today with Delilah."

"But Jeanie," said her master, "I wanted you all to myself today."

Jeanie hung her head. "But it's my birthday, Master, and my day off."

"I guess it can't be helped then," said Master. "But never forget, you were made to serve me."

As Jeanie started to disappear, she heard her master call out, "By the way, Jeanie—Happy Birthday." She smiled.

Jeanie and Delilah materialized at the same time in the restaurant—they caught admiring glances on their way to the table.

Jeanie confided, "Master wanted me to serve him today, and I reminded him that it is my birthday."

"And your day off," said Delilah. "The Union requires masters to give a day off each week."

"Yes," replied Jeanie. "But Master is very old-fashioned and believes I was created to serve him. He doesn't think I should have a life of my own."

"Jeanie," said Delilah, "your master is very *selfish*. The *Union Handbook*, chapter 5, lines 6–8 states, 'Genies are created to serve their masters and also to use their gifts and talents within their communities. Good masters encourage their genies to lead balanced lives.' By the way, have you told him yet about Mr. Paganini?"

There was a long silence. Jeanie hung her head and said quietly, "I don't know how to tell him about Mr. Paganini. He wouldn't understand."

Mr. Paganini was Jeanie's voice teacher. As long as she could remember, Jeanie had wanted to study voice. So with Delilah's encouragement, Jeanie had auditioned for Mr. Paganini. He thought she had great talent, and in return for voice lessons, Jeanie cleaned his house once a week on her day off. She had been taking voice lessons for six months now, and Mr. Paganini had given her the female lead in an upcoming opera production. Only the opera was NOT on one of her days off.

"Maybe I should give up my singing," said Jeanie. "I don't have my master's permission."

"Jeanie," said Delilah, "your voice is a gift. Surely if your master knew about your talent he would want you to share it."

Jeanie wasn't ready to tell Master about her singing lessons or the opera performance. But she continued taking lessons and went to opera rehearsals while Master was at work. Delilah helped her cook and clean so that Master would not guess she was doing other things.

The night of the opera performance arrived.

Just as Jeanie was about to leave, Master arrived home and rubbed her bottle.

"Oh no," thought Jeanie. "I thought Master was working tonight."

"Yes, Master," said Jeanie as she emerged from the bottle, "what is your request?"

"Jeanie, I would like you to join me at the opera tonight. I have been hearing about a wonderful new talent—a woman with a voice like an angel. I want to hear her sing, and I don't want to go alone."

Jeanie thought fast.

"Kind Master," replied Jeanie, "I'm feeling ill tonight. Perhaps Delilah could fill in for me. Would that be acceptable?"

She held her breath, afraid that Master would insist she attend the opera, illness or no illness.

Master said with a sigh, "I'm sorry to hear you aren't feeling well. Please tell Delilah I'll pick her up at 7 p.m., and thank her for taking your place."

Jeanie called Delilah and then headed to the opera house. As she put on her costume and makeup, she thought, "I hope Master won't recognize me like this."

Jeanie sang beautifully, and the opera was spectacular. The audience rendered a thundering ovation as the opera ended, clapping for the new star who sang like an angel. Mr. Paganini gave Jeanie an armful of roses on stage and the curtain came down.

Backstage, Mr. Paganini said, "Jeanie, let's go meet your public. Everyone wants to congratulate you. Here, take my arm and come with me."

Jeanie took Mr. Paganini's arm and they headed out into the theater, where they were quickly surrounded by well-wishers. Oh-oh. There were Delilah and Master.

Master's eyes grew big as he recognized his genie. Delilah quickly exclaimed, "Jeanie, you wanted to introduce Mr. Paganini to Master! Master is so generous to let you use your musical gift to bring such pleasure to others. He is surely proud of you tonight, aren't you Master?"

Mr. Paganini grabbed Master's hand and shook it. He said, "I'm Mr. Paganini. Thank you for being such a kind and generous master. You are wise to permit Jeanie to share her talent. She has such a gift!"

Master was caught a little off guard. What could he say? People were crowding around his genie and her performance had been incredible.

"Thank you, Mr. Paganini. Yes, Jeanie is quite gifted. I am very fond of opera, and it would be wrong for Jeanie to keep such a talent to herself."

"I hope you will continue to allow Jeanie to study voice with me," said Mr. Paganini. "Until tonight, I didn't know she was a genie, but I am even willing to share the cost of her care."

"Master," said Delilah, "I would be pleased to serve you when Jeanie is rehearsing or performing. My master is very liberal and he loves opera, too."

Master agreed to the proposed arrangements, and he and Jeanie returned home.

"Master," said Jeanie, her head down, "forgive me for lying about being ill and hiding my voice lessons. I didn't think you would let me study with Mr. Paganini. You are pretty old-fashioned about such things you know."

She continued, "I hope you will let me continue to train with Mr. Paganini and use my musical gift. I love sharing my talent with others."

"My head is spinning, Jeanie," said her master. "When I saw you on stage and heard you sing I thought, 'She is so beautiful and has the voice of an angel.'"

"Then I thought, 'She looks so familiar. I hope I will get to meet her.' When I saw you up close, I realized you were my very own genie, and I didn't know what to think."

"How do you feel now, Master?" asked Jeanie.

He replied, "I am sad that you did not trust me yet amazed at your talent. Part of me doesn't want to let you serve Mr. Paganini, but I would be selfish to keep you all to myself."

Jeanie gave her master a big hug.

"Shall I perform for you, Master?" asked Jeanie.

"Certainly!" replied her master as he reclined on his favorite sofa.

Jeanie performed for him, singing all his favorite pieces. He closed his eyes and listened, amazed at the richness of her voice.

"What we have been missing out on, Jeanie!" Master exclaimed when she was through. "Perhaps genies are not created *only* to serve their masters. I will be proud to share your talents with the others."

We are all a little like Jeanie and her master when we get stuck in our roles and traditions. What a wonderful thing when we finally step outside our "comfort zones" and share our gifts with others.

THE BOTTOM LINE: Share your talents!

FOOD FOR THOUGHT QUESTIONS

1. How are you like Jeanie?
2. When did you let someone stop you from doing something or try to control your behavior?
3. What are your talents and how do you share them? If you don't share them, why not?
4. Do you need someone like Delilah to encourage you to do your own thing?
5. Describe a time you changed your behavior to please someone else.

13

The Cycle of Abuse

Domestic violence sometimes resembles a dance choreographed from shared history—he makes a move then she makes a countermove. Familiarity and the moves keep the dance going. Each dance partner wears his or her broken-in dance shoes and settles into the practiced rhythm and destructive harmony. The dance of long-term domestic violence is well learned; and even if the partners don't enjoy the actual dance, they are used to the pattern and know all the steps.

Some forms of dance build with the pace and intensity of the music. Slow and steady at first, the dance soon becomes frenzied and more complicated; and there is no time to think. Both partners keep it going, following the steps and staying in rhythm. Passionate feelings override thought and common sense. Their breathing quickens and their hearts pound. They dance to the bitter end.

When the dance is over, the partners are exhausted, sometimes too tired to do anything but sleep. After the music stops, their hearts still pound for a few minutes. It is hard for them to remember the dance or the steps they took. Now that it is over, they are spent from the dance of domestic violence.

To stop the dance of domestic violence, one of the partners must pull away from the dance partner and interrupt the dance, and often the woman must make that first move. When she pulls away, her dance partner may decide that if he can't have her, nobody will. He may not be able to tolerate the injury to his self-centered narcissism. He may try to punish her for leaving and assert control (authority/power). He may do something to prove to her how weak (stupid, inadequate, etc.) she is.

A woman must ultimately decide to keep "dancing" or believe that the benefits of leaving outweigh the losses and risks. She may be reluctant to give up the financial security, the power struggle, having material goods, passionate "make-up" sex, having a place to live, being supported, and having a man in the home for the children.

The wear and tear of the dance of abuse is cumulative, like dancing with torn ligaments, sore feet, and twisted ankles. Women doing the dance of domestic violence need to recognize that it hurts them and others in significant ways.

Chip Away uses a powerful metaphor to address the costs and benefits of staying in an abusive relationship. The author acknowledges that abuse also occurs in same-sex relationships and by women toward men, but in many cultures, male-to-female abuse remains the most common.

CHIP AWAY

If you love a beautiful piece of artwork, you would have loved Stella Statue. She was shapely and well proportioned from her head to her toes, carved many years before out of white marble by a master sculptor. As her marble aged with each passing year, it grew more and more lovely; and her pensive smile matched the sparkle in her eyes. Stella's best friend, Fontana Fountain, lived next door to Stella, and the two of them were enjoying a sunny day in lovely Tuscany, Italy.

Fontana Fountain was made of gray marble, and coins of many shapes and sizes sparkled in the bottom of her watery depths. She had a pet swan in the water next to her, and water flowed freely from the swan's beak back into the fountain. Children and their parents came from miles around to toss coins into the lovely Fontana Fountain and to admire Stella Statue's beauty.

That day, however, Stella was not feeling happy or beautiful. She was trying to keep a tear from escaping and running down her smooth cheeks. Fontana knew Stella better than anyone else in the world and whispered, "OK Stella, what's up? I can tell when something's wrong?"

Stella whispered back, "It's nothing."

Fontana splashed her water a little louder to entertain the children and their parents, and said quietly to her friend, "Come on, what's a friend for if you can't tell her your problems?"

Stella replied, "If you really must know, take a close look at my right cheekbone . . . And my left hip . . . And my upper arms . . . And my tummy . . . "

Fontana looked closely at her friend's body.

"Oh my God, Stella," said Fontana in a horrified voice. "What did Steve do this time?"

Stella could not stop the tears now. They trickled down her cheeks. But none of the people noticed the tears with Fontana spraying mist all around them.

Stella answered. "Steve and I had another fight. He said I had an ugly blemish on my cheek, too much fat on my hip, sagging upper arms, and a fat tummy. He said I was falling apart and he might just find himself a younger girlfriend if I didn't make some changes."

"I told you after the last fight that you would have another fight sooner or later," said Fontana. "And what did you say back to him?"

"Well I got my courage up like you told me to do and said that he needed to love me the way I am." Stella continued, "I also told him he was a sorry old goat and I wasn't going to change for him."

Actually, Steve was a goat, at least half goat. He was a satyr, a creature who was half-goat, half-human. He chased after women and drank too much wine. Stella had been dating him for a long time.

"Good for you," said Fontana. "What did he do next?"

Stella replied, "He said, 'You better watch your mouth—you'll get what's coming to you!' He was really mad. I was proud that I stood up to him, but later in the day, he came back. He brought his chisel and, when no one was looking, he started to chip away at me."

"Chip away?" asked Fontana with dismay.

"Yes," sad Stella sadly. "He took his chisel and started to chip away at the parts of me he doesn't like."

"That's awful," said her friend. "There's no excuse for him putting his hands on you when he's mad! What did you do?"

"I was so shocked that I didn't know what to do," replied Stella. "Steve has been mean before, but he's never chipped away on me like that. Before I even knew what was happening parts of me were flying right and left. I screamed and yelled, but he wouldn't stop."

"Did you call the police?" asked Fontana.

"I could have called the police, but I didn't want to create a disturbance," said Stella.

"He's a scary guy. There's no limit to what he could do to hurt you," warned Fontana.

Stella admitted, "I'm really afraid of him now. He's never been *this* mean. The worst thing he ever did before was call me a bitch because he thought I was flirting with someone."

Stella added, "I'm also really confused."

"I don't know what you're confused about," scoffed Fontana. "It's obvious you need to ditch that guy! And you should have called the police."

"I know you're right," said Stella, "but later, after he cooled down, Steve was so sorry. He cried at what he had done, and he brought me beautiful roses. He says he'll never hurt me again. I think I'm still in love with him."

There were some lovely red roses at the base of Stella's pedestal.

Fontana was angry for her friend. "It doesn't matter if he was nice afterward. And love isn't enough. That old goat should never lay a hand on you. If he tries to hurt you again, *I'm* calling the police. You deserve *better*!"

Fontana was silent for a moment and then added, "You did break up with him, didn't you?"

There was an awkward pause, then Stella answered, "Well, no, I didn't break up with him—he's not that bad, you know. He begged me to forgive him, so I gave him another chance. And the chips were all so little I can cover them with makeup. He can be really nice sometimes, and he had a hard life growing up. He doesn't really know any better."

Fontana just shook her head. "You're following your heart instead of your head, Stella. He's been chipping away at your feelings for a long time. Now he's crossed the line and chipped away at your body. You know he'll do it again!"

Stella didn't want to argue with Fontana. She believed Steve had "learned his lesson" and that he would never hurt her that way again. Fontana didn't know Steve the way Stella did.

It was about two weeks later when Stella had to cancel a date with Steve at the last minute. Her boss had called her into work. She was exhausted when her work shift drew to a close. Then the clock struck 10, and Stella heard a loud, angry voice, "Hey, Stella. Stood me up did you? Look what I have!"

Steve Satyr was drunk and had a beautiful young mermaid on his arm. He shouted, "I told you I would find a younger, more beautiful girlfriend!"

Stella cried out, "I don't know why I stayed with you so long, but Fontana was right—I deserve better. I'm tired of being treated this way by an old drunken goat. Go away and never come back—it's OVER." Stella meant it, at least for the moment. Fontana splashed water on Steve and his date, who galloped off in the other direction.

Steve went away. But at midnight he returned, drunker than before. He had an even larger chisel and a huge sledgehammer. Before Stella could call out, Steve began chipping away—at her face, her arms, her breast, her back.

He sneered, "You think you're really something! You think you're so special! I'll show you!"

Steve moved in for the attack. It was awful, and Fontana was on break, so there was no one to help her.

Stella screamed in her loudest voice, "Police, police, come quickly!"

The police heard Stella's cries and responded, but not quickly enough to prevent harm to Stella. They handcuffed Steve and said, "Don't worry ma'am. He'll be locked up for the next 10 years." One officer took Steve away and locked him up at the local zoo. Another officer offered to escort Stella to the hospital, but she wanted to wait until her friend Fontana returned from break.

When Fontana returned, Stella told her about Steve hurting her again. Fontana looked closely at her friend, whose formerly smooth marble surface was now marred by deep chips and rough edges.

Fontana said sadly, "Stella, I'm so sorry I wasn't here to help. I was afraid that might happen. Abusers want to control others. Steve didn't want to let you go."

Stella admitted, "I wish I had seen that sooner. Sometimes he acted so nice."

Stella didn't want to be alone that night, so Fontana stayed with her. That's what friends are for, you know—they help you through the tough times.

The next morning, Stella asked Fontana, "Do you know a good healer who can fix me—someone with kind, gentle hands?"

Fontana had a friend who was a healer, and she called him. He came right away and for several days he worked skillfully to fix the damaged areas on Stella's body and smooth the rough spots. He also gently explained to Stella that Steve had damaged her soul as well as her body, and the healing of body *and* soul would take a long time. The healer told her to care for herself and to stay away from mean goats.

When the healer had finally finished his work and left, Fontana said, "You know, Stella, men are a little like ice cream. There are lots of flavors to pick from, but you have to figure out which flavors you like best and not overindulge."

"That's true," said Stella with a smile. "But I think I'd rather give up men than ice cream right now."

Stella and Fontana went out for double-dip cones on their next break. There aren't many things more satisfying than the company of a good friend and a double-dip ice cream cone, at least not on a hot summer night.

THE BOTTOM LINE: Don't settle for a mean goat!

FOOD FOR THOUGHT QUESTIONS

1. How are you like Stella?
2. How are you like her friend Fontana?
3. Describe a time you did not object even though someone chipped away at you.
4. Describe a time you gave someone another chance after he or she was rude, threatening, attacking, or aggressive toward you. What was the result?

14

Beyond Sex to Intimacy

Women sexually abused as children sometimes develop altered views of sexuality. Some choose to work as exotic dancers, strippers, prostitutes, or escorts, careers where they experience some perceived *control* over men. However, there is a high rate of STD, sexual exploitation, rape, and re-victimization in those lifestyles. Additionally, women in sexually exploitive jobs or relationships often do not have the educational or financial means to escape the cultures in which they live. Many domestic violence victims were raised in sexist environments in which they and their mothers were belittled and degraded. Some mothers sexually exploit their daughters in return for favors and financial support.

It is not unusual for an abused woman to confuse sex and exploitation with love or intimacy, as she has no template for a healthy, caring relationship. One client reported without batting an eye that she had been with at least 40 sex partners in the prior two years. Her young daughters were put at risk as men came and went in her life. Growing up, she had witnessed the authoritarian control of her father, who later molested her daughters, and submissive dependency of her mother, a prescription drug abuser. The young mother took her first job as a stripper and eventually became an exotic dancer. It is no wonder that she confused sex with intimacy. She did not realize that she had the right to ask for "more" and "better" in her relationships with men, settling for sex as a means of perceived control.

A woman needs to understand that she has choices, but until she loves and fully accepts herself, it is difficult for her to accept the unconditional love of someone else. If a woman then develops the skills and resources (employment, friendships, education, etc.) she needs to live on her own, she may finally have what she needs to risk significant change in her life.

SET YOURSELF FREE

Suzy Sloth was sleepily hanging upside down from a long pole-like tree branch, enjoying a nap in the hot sun at the zoo.

"Psst! Psst!"

Suzy opened one lazy eye and said in a slightly annoyed voice, "Who is that? Can't you see I'm trying to take a nap?"

Again the sound came. "Psst! Psst!"

Suzy opened the other lazy eye. Standing outside her cage was one of the most handsome sloths she had even seen.

"Hi, beautiful," the other sloth flirted. "Why don't you come out and play?"

"Fat chance," said Suzy. "I live in this cage. Why should I leave it? After all, I haven't left it in years!"

"Why not?" asked the other sloth. "There is a wonderful world out here. Why live in a small cage?"

"I lead a simple and easy life," Suzy replied. "Why don't *you* come in and play with me?"

Suzy led a comfortable life. If she saw someone she liked outside her cage, she flirted and maybe even invited the person in for a drink. Later, after having a good time, Suzy fell asleep, and her guest snuck out. Guests never stayed for long. That was Suzy's life: sleeping, eating, and a little entertaining.

Suzy liked her easy life—it was all she had ever known. Someone brought her food every day. Someone filled her water bowl and cleaned her cage. She had a nice branch to hang from. She had friends. She didn't know how to take care of herself, but it didn't matter. Suzy was such a flirt she could get anything she wanted.

But this handsome sloth didn't want to join Suzy in her cage. "You can do better than that," he said. "You deserve better than that. Come *out* and play. I promise I won't bite," he said with a wink and a smile.

He was sure cute. Suzy thought, "Well maybe I could go out on the town just for a few hours." Before she could change her mind, Suzy let herself out of her cage.

"Hi, big guy," flirted Suzy. The sloth just smiled and held paws with her, their four toes entwining. He didn't want to play around—he just wanted to walk and talk and enjoy her company. Suzy was confused.

Suzy wondered, "What does he want? What is he up to?" She wasn't used to a guy being nice and wanting to spend time with her.

So they walked, and talked, and swung from the trees. Around dawn, her new friend said, "Hey Suzy, want to come to my house for the rest of the night instead of going back to the zoo? We need to get some sleep."

"He's just like all the other guys," thought Suzy. "I knew sooner or later he would try to get me into bed."

"Sure," said Suzy. "Let's go to your place." So her friend led her down the path to his tree in the forest. But Suzy's mouth dropped open in astonishment as he climbed onto a tall branch, pulled her up next to him, wrapped her in his arms, and promptly fell asleep.

"He really meant *sleep*," thought Suzy. How strange. It felt nice to be cuddled in his arms, and Suzy put her head on his shoulder and fell asleep beside him.

And that was just the start of going home with him. The next evening when they woke up, the handsome sloth said he wanted Suzy to be part of his life. Suzy decided to stay on, just a day or two longer, out of curiosity of course. A few hours turned into a few days; eventually a few days became a few weeks, then finally a few months. And the sex, when it happened, was out of this world! He took care of her needs first, not like the selfish guys Suzy had entertained in the past.

It was such a different life than Suzy's prior life at the zoo.

"What's on your mind?" her friend often asked. No one had been interested in her mind before. Suzy started reading and learning new things to discuss with her friend.

Suzy's friend took her to lots of new places. They did Yoga, played bingo, and watched TV together. On Saturday nights they went to church. Her friend served her breakfast in bed every Sunday morning. As you can imagine, Suzy and her friend grew very fond of one another.

Then one day, Suzy woke up with an upset stomach and couldn't keep anything down. For the next week, the nausea continued.

"Oh no!" thought Suzy. "I haven't had my cycle in two months. I hope I'm not pregnant." She went to the pharmacy and bought a pregnancy test. Bingo—the line turned blue. She was pregnant.

Suzy was afraid to tell her friend the news. Most male sloths took off when the female got pregnant.

"Oh well," she thought. "It was good while it lasted." It made her sad to think that her friend would probably leave her now that things had changed.

"Hey," she said later that day as she hung upside down in the tree. "It might be time for me to go back to my cage at the zoo." She opened one lazy eye and looked at her friend to see his reaction.

"Why would you want to go back?" he asked.

"Well, I just found out I'm going to be a mother. You probably won't want to hang around me anymore. Most sloths these days want to play around. They aren't the fatherly type." She opened her other lazy eye.

To her surprise, her friend, hanging next to her in the tree, wrapped his long tail around her long tail and said, "You're not going anywhere unless that's what you want. I love you. When I met you, I told you that you deserved better. This is 'better,' don't you think?"

Suzy opened one lazy eye and said, "Yes, this is better. And I love you, too. I think you'll be a great father."

If sloths could smile, Suzy would have smiled. She closed both lazy eyes. It is hard to tell when a sleepy sloth is excited, but the two curling tails might have given you a clue. Leaving her cage had given Suzy a whole new life. She did deserve better.

THE BOTTOM LINE: Free yourself from what cages you in!

FOOD FOR THOUGHT QUESTIONS

1. How are you like Suzy?
2. List men who have cared for you but did not expect sex in return.
3. Identify five things a man would like about you that have nothing to do with your appearance or sex.
4. What do you think it means when someone says, "You deserve more"? Do you believe it?

Part III

STORIES FOR PREPARATION

Women that plan to make a significant change within a month have entered the Preparation Stage of Change. They have been testing the water in their relationships and they see the potential value in making a change. At this point of the change process, clients come to see that the benefits of change will outweigh the risks.

In this stage, the therapist needs to help the client remove barriers to change. There is a focus on encouragement, self-efficacy, making plans, and setting goals. The stories selected for this phase of treatment help women clearly articulate the problems in their relationships, intensify emotion about maltreatment, increase righteous indignation, and clarify the steps they will go through in the change process.

The stories in this section will lead a woman through the Preparation Phase. They encourage her to take her time, have the right tools, and be patient. They warn the woman of codependent attitudes and educate her about fight or flight. The stories prepare the woman to enter the Action Phase and help her be ready to pursue her goals.

15

The Powerful Pull of the Past

A woman presented for outpatient treatment with somatic complaints, severe anxiety and sleep problems, mood swings, and significant memory impairment. We knew she had been severely abused and neglected as a child and teen, including sexual trauma. She had been in an abusive relationship with a partner for the prior 15 years and was having trouble leaving that relationship.

Her partner was like a persistent riptide, pulling her back over and over again into a self-destructive lifestyle. His *riptide currents* were strong and powerful—threats, demeaning criticism, seductiveness, drugs, and angry cruelty. He had the ability to go inside her and *pull* out the wounded parts of her from her past that still lived. At the time she entered treatment, she was largely unaware of the degree to which her past was impacting her adult life.

An early sign we had of her fragmented self was when her therapist confronted her in a session about her short-tempered behavior with her young children. She became fearful, apologetic, and childlike and hid her face against the wall. In another session, she voiced confusion and anger that *someone* had come into her apartment and *messed with* her things over the weekend. She also brought in a journal with different handwritings and began to have more awareness of some split-off parts of herself.

What became clear was that until she became more aware of these sides of herself, her abusive partner would continue to pull for her weakest sides. When he was threatening or cruel, the abused child inside her displayed fear and helplessness. When he was seductive or manipulative, a wild, angry *teenage* side emerged. When he was critical and demeaning, a co-dependent woman knew how to please him and prove herself worthy. And most of the time, a very kind, wise, playful mother attended therapy sessions, wanting to become stronger and live her own life yet pulled strongly by the riptide of her past.

This story is to be used during the Preparation (or early Action) Phase of treatment. It can be used for any woman whose past trauma is tugging at her and pulling her into relationships that recapitulate past relational issues. It is best used when a woman starts to become aware of the pull of the past, to help her get in touch with the ways in which her emotions, especially fear, anger, and loneliness, prevent her from outsmarting the riptide of past abuse.

A SAFE PLACE TO CALL HOME

There once was a woman who really needed a *safe place* to call home. As far back as she could remember she had lived in awful places with mean people.

When she was little, she lived with her parents—you would not believe the horrible, *unspeakable,* nearly unbearable things she had suffered at the hands of her parents. Most of it she didn't even remember, because it happened when she was very young. But trust me—her parents did things to that little girl that no child should ever experience.

On her eighth birthday, her grandmother took her in. Grandma might have reminded you of a Disney villain—you know, the one in *Sleeping Beauty* who made the princess prick her finger and go into a deep sleep; or the stepmother in *Cinderella* who made Cinderella work while her own daughters lived in luxury; or maybe even the nasty queen in *Snow White*, who was so jealous and tricked Snow White to eat the poisoned apple. I guess you get the picture—Grandma, just like the others, pretended to be nice but when no one was looking she turned into a selfish, mean, wicked witch.

After the girl was sent away from her grandmother's house at age 12, she lived in a string of foster homes. Her foster parents got frustrated with her when she started to show her hurt and anger from the past; but of course they expected her to act her age and be nice. They did not understand her behavior and accused her of lying about things. One after another, they gave up on her.

Then the woman finally grew up on the outside (but not completely on the inside) and it was time for her to live her own life; but she didn't really know how to do that. She ended up living with mean men who did some of the same things to her as her parents, her grandmother, and her foster parents. They called her names, hurt her, expected her to act her age and wanted her to put up with their selfishness. She did not realize yet that she deserved better, so she put up with their treatment and just felt worse and worse about herself.

It was a small miracle, but the woman finally left a relationship with a very mean man and moved into her own house. It was a small house with little rooms and thick walls; and most of the bedrooms had strong locks on the doors. The woman didn't have a key to open the locked doors so she just lived in the rooms that were open to her. She also did not quite feel safe in the house. She heard noises at night and what sounded like voices coming from the locked rooms and it gave her the creeps. Sometimes she thought she was losing her mind.

For many nights, the woman did not sleep well. Then one night, a voice coming from behind one of the locked doors woke her from a sound sleep.

"You stupid bitch!" shouted the voice. In a very weird way the voice sounded both like her father and like the mean man with whom she had lived. "You deserve what you got! You won't ever amount to anything."

The woman got out of bed and crept down the hall. She stopped outside the locked door where the voice was coming from. She knocked, and waited.

"Go on, bitch," said the voice. "Open the door and let me out."

"I don't have the key," said the woman. "And you sound too mean. I don't want to let you out."

"You would be mean, too, bitch, if you had gone through what I've gone through in my life. And I'm going to make your life miserable until you let me out."

"Well I'm not letting you out," said the woman. "If you want to talk to me, it will have to be from behind this locked door."

At that, the woman ran back down the hall to her bedroom, muttering to herself, "There's no such thing as ghosts . . . There's no such things as ghosts . . ." She then locked herself in her bedroom, put thick earplugs in her ears, and got back in bed. She thought, "I have always had such a vivid imagination. I must have been dreaming." The woman went back to sleep after saying this at least 100 times.

I know, you are probably saying, "That is really weird shit," but it is the truth.

A few hours later, the woman awoke again from a deep sleep. This time, even with the earplugs, she heard a girl's voice pleading from one of the other locked bedrooms down the other hallway.

"Let me out—let me out! I'll be good, I promise. I don't mean to be bad. I swear I'm telling the truth. Here, I'll cut a switch and you can whoop me. Please don't leave me alone in this dark closet."

The woman was not as scared this time as she unlocked her bedroom door and crept down the hall. When she reached the locked door where the voice was pleading, she knocked and called out.

"Who is in there? What is wrong?"

"You know me," said the girl's voice. "Please let me out."

"I can't let you out—I don't have the key—and I don't know you," said the woman. "If you want to talk to me you will have to do it from behind this locked door. And you sound too young to be awake so late at night."

"I'm ten years old," replied the girl. "And I'm usually awake at night. That's when I get most scared."

"What are you scared of?" asked the woman.

"I'm not ready to tell you that," the girl answered. "But maybe I will when I'm ready."

So the woman told the girl goodnight and ran down the hallway to her room, saying, "There's no such thing as ghosts. I must be dreaming."

She went in her bedroom, locked her door, and went back to sleep after telling herself at least 100 times that she was not losing her mind.

A couple of hours later a very different voice awoke her from the deepest sleep yet. It was a young child's voice, screaming and crying in fear and pain.

"It hurts when he does that. I'm sorry I wet my pants. I'm sorry I cried. I promise to be good. Just make him stop hurting me!"

The woman ran down the hallway at the sound of the very young child's voice.

She knocked and called through the door, "Please don't cry. I won't let him hurt you. No one is here but you and me. You're safe."

The child's voice cried out, "No one is safe behind a locked door in a dark room! Please let me out!"

"I'm so sorry," said the women, with sadness in her heart. She really wanted to let the young child out. She knew the child had been treated very badly and her voice sounded hurt and scared. The woman felt a strange kinship with the child and did not want to leave her all alone in a dark, locked room.

"But I don't have a key to this room," the woman said to the child. "We will have to talk through the locked door. Please come close to the door and sit against it. I am right here on the other side. I will stay here as long as you need me, until you can get back to sleep. And I promise I won't let him hurt you."

The very young child continued to whimper for awhile but the woman comforted her and sang her a lullaby and told her nice fairy tales with happy endings. She had the child pretend she was in a safe, magical place with all the things she ever wanted. She ended with, "There now, I'm wrapping my arms around you in a big, safe hug. Let's rock together in a nice rocking chair—it's time for both of us to go back to sleep. I promise I'll be here when you wake up in the morning." And so they spent the rest of the night.

The next morning, the woman woke up knowing what she had to do to finally be living in a safe place to call home. She had to open her home up—no more small rooms with thick walls, and no more talking through locked doors. Before she could become nervous, she called a contractor to begin the remodeling.

You would never believe what that house was like when the remodel was complete. The woman finally felt she had a place to call home. The workpersons had built a big great room at the center of the house. It was very open and light shone in from the windows. There was a long wooden table at one end of the great room, big enough to seat ten. And at the other end there were soft couches, a double swing that hung from the ceiling, and a hammock to rest in that swung gently back and forth. There was a huge rocking chair and many types of art and playthings. There was music playing inside and out; and the garden behind the house had wind chimes, fountains, and pretty flowers. There was a hot tub in the deck and a shallow pool with a waterfall. Inside the house, there were also two large bedrooms with big, safe beds.

And if you were wondering, the mean-voiced person behind the first door knew where the key was all along—so she confessed and the woman unlocked the doors. The woman, the girl, and the child were finally able to gather at the table to talk.

As you might guess, each of the persons that came to the table had very important things to share—feelings and memories that had been unspoken for far too long.

I hope that you have a safe place to call home—everyone, no matter what, deserves that.

THE BOTTOM LINE: Find a safe place to call home!

FOOD FOR THOUGHT QUESTIONS

1. How are you like the woman in this story?
2. When do you feel most safe?
3. What would your safe house look like? You might want to draw it.
4. If it was your voice behind each of the doors, how old would you be and what would you be saying?
5. When you imagine sitting around the long wooden safe table to talk, what would you most need to talk about? Would you want anyone else at the table?

16

Having the Right Tools

Survival Skills

We can't expect people to change when they lack the basic *tools* to do so. Asking a woman to leave the only life she has known without any *survival tools* is like asking her to climb an ice-covered mountain barefoot and alone. A woman must have a good *toolbox* to become self-sufficient and leave an abusive partner—somewhere to go, the means to support herself and her children, and a number of community supports. Without a car, income, and friends, an isolated abuse victim may believe that leaving is not possible.

So what kinds of tools can we offer? Things like vocational rehabilitation or job training for those that lack job skills, transportation, food stamps, case management, clothing to wear for a job hunt, access to educational resources, affordable access to mental health treatment, and child care.

Many adult victims of domestic violence have been "on their own" since childhood, trying to survive without needed resources. One such woman was homeless and jobless, trying to reunify with her children following a lengthy hospitalization. She was a survivor of childhood trauma, had severe mental illness with secondary drug abuse, and had put her children repeatedly at risk. The local social services department did not understand that expecting her to "pull herself up by her bootstraps," without support and resources, was like throwing someone in a rough ocean without a life raft. The story that follows will help clients think about resources they need to be truly successful in their quest for self-sufficiency.

CLIMBING ICE MOUNTAIN

No one would ask you to swim the English Channel without knowing how to swim! And even if you were a great swimmer, you would never start such a swim without a warm, waterproof wetsuit, food, drinking water, a flashlight, and a good boat to rest in when you became tired.

So you will be surprised at what the children in this story were trying to do, all by themselves, in the dead of winter. It was January in Iceville, which means −20° temperatures, usually sunny skies, and ice crystals sparkling like diamonds on all the trees. Everything in Iceville stays frozen November through March, but those that live there love it.

That particular morning a group of tourists was sightseeing. Of course there was not much to see except white smoke rising from most chimneys and sparkling ice on the ground and trees. The tourists were on their way to Ice Mountain, the highest peak in Iceville, known for its shiny, bluish white ice-coated sides. If you rode the aerial tramway to the top, there was a gift shop and a counter where you could buy hot apple cider. There was also a large fireplace where you could warm your hands and rocking chairs by the fire. Everyone that visited Iceville went to Ice Mountain.

As the tourists approached the tram entrance, they heard voices coming from the base of Ice Mountain.

"Let's try again."

There were four young children standing at the foot of the mountain. They looked about ten, eight, six, and five years old. One was wearing shorts and none had on winter coats. They had no winter boots on their feet, in fact three of them were wearing flip-flops, and the oldest child had on sandals. As the tourists came near, they saw the oldest child take a running start and slip-slide about four feet up the icy slope, only to slide right back down.

"Crap!" they heard her say. The tourists laughed at the spectacle. The girl saw them and said, embarrassed, "Sorry for my language."

"That's all right," said one of the tourists. "But what are you doing?"

"We're climbing Ice Mountain," said the oldest girl.

The tourist replied, "Climbing Ice Mountain? You have no equipment, and you'll freeze to death before you reach the top. Where is your mother?"

The youngest child replied, "She is in bed with the flu."

The next oldest child added, "She told us not to wake her up."

The second oldest stated, "I asked her what we were supposed to do while she rested."

And the oldest child continued, "She said she didn't care what we did."

"Yah," said the youngest. "Mom said, 'I ache all over and I have a fever. You can climb Ice Mountain as far as I'm concerned, but whatever you do, don't wake me up.'"

"That's right," agreed the oldest. "So that's what we're doing. But it's not working very well—too slippery. And if we go home and wake up Mom, there's going to be big trouble."

The tourist suggested, "I'm sure your mother didn't really mean for you to climb Ice Mountain—you would need warm clothes, adult supervision, and the right equipment."

"Well," said the children. "Could you get us some clothes and equipment so we can climb the mountain? We have always wanted to do it."

"I guess we could," said the adults, because of course they did not want the children to wake up their flu-ridden, sleeping mother.

Working together, the adults and children came up with a marvelous list of what they would need to make the climb:

- Snow boots with ice cleats, lined with waterproof wool
- Wool socks
- Ropes to tie the children together as they climbed and keep them from falling
- Pulleys to pull them up the mountain side with the ropes
- Spiked steps to pound into the ice
- A mallet to pound in the spiked steps
- Down-filled ski jackets with warm hoods
- Down-filled gloves
- Water-repellant ski suits
- High-energy snacks

Half the adults went to the top of the mountain to pull the children up; and the other half went to the bottom to catch them and keep them safe if they slipped and fell. They even set up a trampoline at the bottom just in case someone got past an adult.

It was a glorious day to climb, sunny and cold. The children decided to climb the side of the mountain with no trees—just solid, beautiful, bluish-white ice as far as you could see. Warmly dressed and tied together, they drove their boot cleats into the ice and climbed from one spiked step to the next. An adventurous adult tourist had hammered in the steps for them. He had insisted that he be the first climber, to guide the children and ensure their safety. The pulleys helped, as when the climbers grew tired, the people at the top pulled them up using the ropes. No one even fell, so the trampoline was left in place for the following summer.

"Hurray!" shouted the group as they pulled up the last small red-cheeked climber who had grown tired halfway up.

They all warmed their hands by the fire and enjoyed hot chocolate and cider before taking the aerial tramway back down. The children waved goodbye to their new friends and headed home. They shushed one another as they entered the house, then put their wet clothes in the dryer, and sat down to watch TV just as their mother came into the room.

"You were so quiet," she said with a kind smile. "I'm feeling a little better after my long day in bed. What did you do with yourselves while I rested?"

"We climbed Ice Mountain," said the youngest, "like you said."

The mother laughed, not believing the child. "No, really, what did you do all day?" she asked.

The oldest child gave the others a look that said, "Be quiet. She would never believe us anyway," and answered, "Oh, just a little of this and a little of that. We kept quiet so that you could rest."

But now a word of caution—readers should never try this on their own even if they should someday visit Iceville. The children in the story broke quite a few rules, you know, *including never go with strangers* and *never climb a mountain without your mother's permission*. After all, climbing Ice Mountain is dangerous even under the best of circumstances.

I like to think that after climbing the mountain, the children knew that they could do just about anything successfully if they had the right tools. I hope you know that, too.

THE BOTTOM LINE: With the right tools, you can do anything!

FOOD FOR THOUGHT QUESTIONS

1. List the things that would have to change for a woman to get out of a bad relationship.
2. Good relationships require interpersonal skills (tools). What tools do you already have? What do you need?
3. What tools does a woman need when she is in an abusive relationship?

17

Facing Your Own Monsters

In the early 1990s, I heard Bill O'Hanlon paraphrase the novel *A Wizard of Earthsea* by Ursula K. Le Guin. The story and its metaphors captivated me and I have shared it with friends, supervisees, and clients. The story is about self-acceptance, that is, embracing all parts of ourselves, even parts we fear or dislike. It is about facing the consequences of one's own actions and the impossibility of trying to run from or kill off those things in ourselves that we judge to be shameful or destructive.

The process of the therapeutic relationship helps clients integrate their various "parts." I remember O'Hanlon describing a session that took place with a client ashamed of her past—she considered some things "too awful to talk about." She felt that she had changed and wanted to leave those parts of her behind. He suggested that excluding parts of her past was like serving a pie with a piece or two missing and calling it "whole." He encouraged her to acknowledge and affirm all the pieces of her pie.

Russian nesting dolls (can be purchased online) are my clinical parallel to O'Hanlon's pie. I hand them to clients, and as they take them apart, we talk about other ages and stages that lie within, sides of the self that have been hidden or put aside yet continue to affect the person's functioning. What follows is my own simpler version of the monster story. We all need to embrace the past (and what we fear within ourselves) in our quest for wholeness.

THE MONSTER WITHIN

It was an ugly, smelly, pimply-faced monster that emerged from the tip of the young wizard's wand. It towered over the boy, and as it snorted in his face, yellow-green globs of mucus splattered on those close by that watched in horror. The monster grinned, shouting, "Free at last!" while the villagers screamed and ran frantically off in all directions. A cold, stiff wind had crawled inside their bones, and the time of peace as they had known it had passed.

"What have you done?" asked a wise old wizard as he stepped out of a low-hanging cloud and approached the young man.

The young wizard hung his head. How many times had his mentor warned him? He could hear the master's words.

"You are talented, descended from a long line of wizards. Someday you will lead us all, but until then, respect your power. Some magic is still beyond you, and there is much you do not yet understand. You have the power to create and the power to destroy. Strive to use your gifts wisely."

The young wizard had studied with the master ever since the Glow had come upon him three years prior. When the power of the Glow comes upon a wizard, it is a sign that the magic has chosen him to lead. It is his Destiny.

At first, the young wizard studied the magic day and night, for he did not yet fully understand what lay within him and the power of his wand. There was much to learn—a different magic for all things. Out of great respect, he listened to the master's every word, and he practiced diligently so that the master might find him deserving of the Glow

Yet a change started to come over the young wizard as he grew taller and stronger, entering the time when a boy becomes a young man. He had his eye on a pretty girl and often grew tired of studying. He even dared question his destiny. "Why am I doing this? There is too much to learn, and I'm never going to be able to master it. I want to be like other young wizards and have a life of my own, but all I get to do is study. It's not fair."

The young wizard didn't yet realize that the Glow was not about fairness—it was about destiny. His maturity and wisdom of course did not match his height, and he became ever more impetuous and impatient.

More and more, the young wizard gave into his impatience. He started taking long breaks when he should have been studying and skipped important parts of his lessons. "I know enough," he told himself. "I can learn the rest later."

He pretended to be working hard but snuck out to mix and mingle with the other young wizards. He started drinking wizard nectar at night and awoke late in the day, grumpy and tired. Then one day, the pretty girl came to visit him, and the young wizard wanted to show off his special powers. He turned to a page in the magic book that was far beyond his current level of training.

"Let me show you what I can do!" he bragged to the girl. She smiled admiringly at him as he drew his wand and started reading the words of the spell. He was down to the last word when he stopped.

"Hmm . . ." The last word was one he could not pronounce. And there were instructions for a wand movement he had not yet learned.

He thought, "I'm not sure how to pronounce that one word. Is it Afflicto-CHUS or AfflictoSHUS? And am I supposed to twist the wand up and to the right or down and to the left? Oh well, it probably won't really matter."

He called out loudly with confidence, "AFFLICTOSHUS!" as he twisted his wand down and to the left.

And that is when the monster appeared out of the tip of his wand. Pretty big mistake, I would say . . .

The master appeared from within a dark cloud and said, "Now you will face the consequences of your actions. You have acted on the impulse of youth and used magic far beyond your ability. This is a monster of your own making and until you figure out what you MUST do, darkness will follow you and all those around you."

The young wizard begged the master with fear in his voice, "Please make the monster go away. Surely you can fix this and right my wrong."

"No," said the master, "this time only you can right your wrong. The monster is part of you." And with that he disappeared back into the dark cloud from which he had come.

The young wizard did what anyone else would do when confronted by a dangerous monster—he ran off in fear to escape and hide. But wherever he went, the monster sniffed him out and followed. "I am a monster of your own making!" he sneered. "I am part of you and you cannot hide from me—you will never escape me!"

It was true. From village to village, the monster pursued the young wizard, bellowing loudly. Along the way, the monster impaled villagers on his long spiked claws and tossed them like puppets to the sky. His fiery breath destroyed everything in his path. Wherever he went, dark clouds followed, and he wreaked havoc and terror on the formerly peaceful valley.

The young wizard, who had found a place to hide in a cave deep in the hills, agonized over what the master had said. "What is it I MUST do?" he questioned. "What did he mean?"

Then an idea suddenly came to him.

"He is part of me. I can't hide from him, so I will call him out and kill him, even if I die in the process. That is surely what I MUST do. And once I destroy him, then he will be gone for good."

So the young wizard left the cave, calling out, "Monster, Monster! Come and fight me!" He shouted loudly, pretending to be brave, as he walked to the foot of the valley, which was cloaked in darkness.

The monster of course was there, waiting for him.

"Come get me, Monster," called out the young wizard, and his hands shook in fear as he drew his wand. It is a brave and terrifying thing to face your own death before you are old and gray.

"Rrr!" bellowed the monster as it slowly moved toward him. "I've been waiting for you!"

"Enough is enough!" declared the wizard. "My magic has harmed so many innocent people and wreaked havoc on the entire kingdom. I will destroy you if it is the last thing I do!" He moved toward the monster, his wand drawn, ready to fight.

The monster was close enough for the wizard to see the green-yellow mucus in his nostrils and feel the fiery heat from his cavernous mouth.

The monster laughed. "You are a foolish boy! I'm a monster of your own making. I am part of you. You can't destroy me."

"But I will try!" answered the boy who continued to move toward the monster.

And then, just as the boy was ready to cast a spell to destroy the horrible monster, the voice of the master spoke clearly in his head.

"He is a monster of your own making. He is part of you. You cannot hide from him and you cannot destroy him. You know what you MUST do."

And in that moment, the young wizard knew what he MUST do. He opened his arms wide, rushed forward to meet the monster, and howled out loudly with all the grief, remorse, pain, and fear he carried inside him. The wizard wrapped his arms around the monster in a fierce embrace and their eyes met with forgiveness and humility.

Then with a "POOF" the monster was gone, back into the young wizard, and the darkness passed from the valley.

"Well done," said the master as he appeared next to the boy. "You learned the truth, something I could not teach you. We cannot hide from our monsters and we cannot kill them. They are part of us. Only by facing and embracing the monster of your own making could you once again be whole."

From that day forward, the young wizard respected the master and worked *mostly* within the limits of his magic. I wish I could say he never again became impatient or made mistakes; and sometimes he went a *little bit ahead* in the book of spells—but with no worse results than turning a crystal ball into rubber and making deodorant that smelled like shit. He had learned that when he made decisions that hurt him or others, the only thing to do was face them and know that they were part of his destiny.

THE BOTTOM LINE: Embrace your monsters!

FOOD FOR THOUGHT QUESTIONS

1. What is your monster?
2. When do you run and hide?
3. When do you fight for survival?
4. What would it mean for you to "embrace" your monster?

18

Identifying and Expressing Feelings

Women involved in abusive relationships do things to *keep peace* and avoid harm. Some tune out or dissociate when there are threats of or actual violence, the numbness a means of self-protection. They remain watchful and vigilant, trying not to make waves. Other women are *fighters* and respond with verbal or physical counterviolence to the partner. Both types of women feel sadness, fear, hurt, and loss at the hands of their partners; each trying to find a way to tolerate what is happening rather than face abandonment.

Scientists now know that chronic abuse can damage the brain and endocrine system, leading to problems with emotional control (McCollum, 2006). Abuse victims may develop symptoms such as denial or repression ("I'm not mad"), dissociation ("tuning out"), somatic complaints ("I'm not mad, I'm sick"), rage ("I'll get back at him if it's the last thing I do—he deserves it!"), rationalization ("if the kids would stop yelling, he wouldn't get mad"), stoicism ("I'll stay for the kids"), and hopelessness ("he's right, I would never be able to live without him").

As they begin treatment, many women need help identifying and expressing feelings. Traumatized women often use avoidance or denial to cope with their feelings—they don't want to "go crazy" by letting out their feelings, so they don't "go there" at all.

One client said, "I don't let myself think about it. I can't talk about it. If I let it out, I would lose it—I might kill him." She compared her "letting it out" to a destructive flood that would overwhelm her, instead of a carefully planned release of water through a dam. She feared she would drown in the pain of an out-of-control flood.

A *Little at a Time* is a humorous story about Elly Elephant, who has stored up too much *shit* and bad feelings. As a result, she has become immobilized. She learns to open up and let her feelings, and *shit*, out a little at a time. Women can learn to do the same.

*When reading the story with teens or children, the word *poop* may be substituted for *shit*.

A LITTLE AT A TIME

Four-year-old Eleanor Elephant could not move. No, she was not paralyzed or injured. She had lived at the Louisville Zoo since she was two years old. It was a nice place with smelly straw (from elephant dung, of course), shade trees, and water. People came from miles around to watch the elephants walk and play, but Elly just lay there by a pool of water.

"Come on, Elly," people called out. "Get up and play. Get up and run around. Get up and squirt water on the other elephants."

But Elly just lay there.

The other elephants enjoyed their life. They lumbered around slowly, except when they got excited, mad, or very playful. But Elly did not move at all—she was too big.

Was she *fat*, you ask? Not really. She was big and round and puffed up like a balloon.

You see, Elly was full of "shit," or, in elephant terms, dung. She had held in her shit for two whole years, and two years of elephant shit is a lot of shit! Most people know what it feels like to hold in shit. It gets harder, and then it hurts to let it out, so you stop trying. Then your belly starts to hurt and gas builds up. Eventually you can't go at all, even if you try.

Elly started holding in her shit at the same time she started holding in her *bad feelings*; feelings like *fear, sadness, anger,* and *worry.* Elly didn't want her shit, or her feelings, to come out all at once in a big smelly, painful mess, so she kept it all in.

That is why Elly couldn't move. The other elephants and the zookeeper offered to help, but Elly said, "I don't want or need your help. My life is fine, thank you. My life and my shit are none of your business!"

But one day, an older elephant said, "Elly, you need to get up and get a life."

Elly admitted, "I would like to. But I'm too full of shit and can't move."

"You need to let it out, your shit and your feelings," said the older friend.

Elly said, "It will all come out at once, and it will be too smelly and hurt too much!"

"Elly," replied her friend. "Don't you know that you need to let it out *a little at a time*?"

"A little at a time?" asked Elly.

"Yes," said her friend. "Feelings and shit kept inside too long are hard to let out. When you let them out a little at a time, you start to feel better."

Elly thought, "Letting it out is not going to work. I just know it will hurt. I just know it will all come out at once and make a big mess."

Elly didn't want to hurt her friend's feelings by saying those things.

"OK," said Elly. "I'll try. But I don't think I'll be able to stand on my own two feet."

Elly's friend trumpeted loudly to the other elephants. "Heads up, might need some help here. Elly's ready to stand up and deal with her shit."

"You can do it!" encouraged two other elephants as they lumbered toward Elly and her friend.

Working together, all of the elephants in the yard helped Elly get up off the ground until she was standing on her own two feet. She wobbled a little but stayed standing.

"Come on, Elly," they cried out. "It's time to get moving!" Her friend stood beside her to offer support.

"I don't think I can do this," said Elly. "I can't walk."

"Baby steps," said her friends. "Just take baby steps, one step at a time."

Elly took a careful step forward, then another. One step—two. One step—two.

"I'm walking again!" trumpeted Elly in an excited voice.

Elly moved slowly away from the pool, with everyone cheering.

"Come on, Elly," they shouted, smiling. "You can do it!"

Elly's friend whispered in her ear, "Get ready, Elly. You'll probably start feeling things inside now that you are moving."

You might smile at what happened next.

"Faaaaaaaaaaart!" went Elly. It was a *big one*!

"Oh my goodness!" said Elly, a little embarrassed, as her face turned bright red. "Excuse me!"

"It's OK," everyone said. "That's going to happen as things get moving."

As Elly walked around the elephant yard, with the help of her friends, she started letting her feelings, and her shit, out a little at a time. The zookeeper came to the elephant yard to help.

"Shit-shit," went Elly. "Shovel-shovel," went the zookeeper. You know, the zookeeper has to clean up the elephant yard, and this was going to be a big clean-up job!

It went on for four days and four nights.

Elly cried, and laughed, and raged, and shivered, and shook as she let out her shit and her feelings, a little at a time. Her belly got smaller and smaller. Her legs grew stronger and stronger. Elly felt much better inside.

"Hip, hip, hooray for Elly!" cheered the people.

After that, Elly started letting her shit and her feelings out every day, a little at a time. For Elly, that meant no build up, no pain, and no smelly leaking shit. She was sometimes tempted to hold strong feelings in, but holding in feelings has a pain of its own.

People came for miles around to take rides in a little chair on Elly's back and to watch her squirt water on the other elephants. Elly waved her trunk at the people and trumpeted in a loud, proud voice.

Elly was proud that she had conquered her problem, but she was also proud for another reason. She kept the zookeeper so busy shoveling shit that his job was secure for years to come!

THE BOTTOM LINE: Let it out, a little at a time!

FOOD FOR THOUGHT QUESTIONS

1. How are you like Elly?
2. What have you stored up that you need to let out?
3. What are you afraid will happen if you let it out?
4. What would help you let things out a little at a time?

19

Change Takes Time

We live in a world where a "quick fix" is valued over patient hard work. Many people seek immediate gratification through shopping, gambling, cutting, exercise, sex, drugs, alcohol, and food—all these and more can become mood-altering "highs" to relieve uncomfortable mood states such as boredom, depression, sadness, anxiety, loneliness, or anger.

It is important for a woman to recognize the intense, uncomfortable feelings that are hard for her to tolerate—instead of seeking a quick fix, she needs to accept, perhaps even welcome, those feelings and figure out what they are telling her. Intense mood states pass, and therapists can help clients develop coping skills to tolerate strong negative emotion.

Women who experience intense, negative moods may be encouraged to keep a journal to track their mood states and find connections among life events, thoughts, feelings, and behaviors rather than seeking an easy way out. DBT, ACT, and mindfulness interventions can be helpful treatment modalities. DV victims need to become less "set" in their ways and more flexible in their solutions, as after concrete hardens, it is quite messy to "fix" any mistakes.

One woman called often in *crisis*, not realizing that her impulsive choices and behaviors had precipitated the crisis. One focus of therapy was to help her see the possible long-term benefits of other choices.

The "quick fix" cycle is hard to break. The humorous story that follows is guaranteed to provide food for thought.

THE QUICK FIX

Deidre Duck waddled into the hardware store in Rochester, New York, and quacked loudly, "Quee-yick, Quee-yick, y'all, ahh nee-yed sum hay-yelp!" A couple of children giggled and were quickly "shushed" by their mother. You might think they were giggling at seeing a duck in a hardware store, but that was not the case. New York stores do not discriminate against ducks, so you often see them in hardware stores.

"Mom," said one child, "I can't tell if she's saying 'Quack' or 'Quick.' She talks funny!"

"She's saying, 'Quick, quick, I need some help,'" said the mother. "She's from somewhere down South and has an accent."

The child's mother was right. Deidre was from Simpsonville, South Carolina, and she had a Southern drawl.

"It's OK, Ma'am," said Deidre. "I'm new to New York." Only the way she said it sounded like, "Ah'm neyoo teeoo Neyoo Yo-walk."

The children giggled again, but one tugged on her mother's shirt. "Let's help her, Mom."

The mother went over to Deidre and asked in a friendly voice, "Can we help you?"

Deidre said, "Mah nayem iz Dayeedrah. Ahh bawt sum qwiyick sayet con-craite, fow-wur a neyoo sahdwawk ayand drahvweigh. It dihdint wohk ayand ah wahnt mah muhnee bay-ack," meaning, "My name is Deidre. I bought some quick set concrete for a new sidewalk and driveway. It didn't work and I want my money back."

You can add the accent for the rest of the story if you like, but from this point on, I'll just write in a way that you clearly understand what Deidre said.

"Hmm," said the mother, "You need to talk to the store clerk. I can translate for you. By the way, my name is Pat."

Pat took Deidre to the store clerk and said, "This duck bought some quick mix, quick hardening concrete and says it didn't work right."

The clerk said, "Tell me what happened."

Deidre said, "I mixed the concrete just like the bag said. I poured the sidewalk, one square at a time. Later that day there were strange marks all over the concrete—it looks terrible!"

She continued, "The same thing happened with the driveway when I poured it the next day. After it hardened there were strange marks all over it, like cracks."

The store clerk was concerned—maybe there was something wrong with the quick mix, quick hardening concrete. The clerk suggested she could go look at Deidre's sidewalk and driveway.

Deidre only lived two blocks away. Pat, her children, and the store clerk walked to Deidre's house and she showed them her new sidewalk and driveway.

There were marks all over the concrete. The clerk and Pat looked carefully at the sidewalk and each said, "I've never seen marks like those in concrete before! What could have caused them?"

As they stared, one of Pat's children giggled and tugged on her shirt.

"There you go giggling again," said Pat. "What's so funny now?"

"Mom," said the child. "I know what those marks are. They're duck feet prints. Deidre must have walked on the wet concrete before it dried."

The child saw what the adults were unable to see. She was right, as children often are. There were duck-feet prints all over the sidewalk and driveway.

"Deidre," asked Pat, "Did you walk on the concrete while it was wet? Before it was hard and dry?"

Deidre quacked back, "Of course I walked on it—that's why I used 'Quick set, quick dry concrete!' I was tired of waddling on dirt and rocks."

"How long did you wait before you walked on it?" Pat asked.

"I counted to 100 after I poured each section, because that is the highest I can count, and then I walked on it to pour the next section."

Pat replied, "Well, you are supposed to wait at least an hour. Sometimes it takes up to 24 hours to set. You can't walk on it any sooner."

"Nonsense!" said Deidre with a smile. "I can't wait that long for anything. I'm always in a hurry and like a quick fix."

"Well," said Pat. "When you go after a quick fix, you have to live with the results. No one can help you if you ignored instructions. Some things are worth waiting for."

It was true. Some things are worth waiting for and require hard work and patience. You may laugh at Deidre because her behavior seems so ridiculous. Deidre was going to have to live with duck-feet prints on her concrete, just as you have to live with the consequences of your impulsive decisions. For her it was concrete—for you, well only you know . . . One thing is for sure—she had the most interesting sidewalk and driveway of anyone in Rochester, New York.

THE BOTTOM LINE: Some things are worth waiting for!

FOOD FOR THOUGHT QUESTIONS

1. When are you most impatient?
2. Give an example of a time you were in a hurry for something to change.
3. What does it mean to say, "Change takes time"?

20

Codependency

Codependent persons take care of or help others at their own expense. It is not a bad thing to help others; but it is not good to ignore or minimize one's own needs. It is also not a good thing to allow others to walk all over, take advantage of, or put down one's own self. In families with substance abuse or domestic violence, for example, persons' needs/rights are too often violated or ignored. It is OK to value yourself as much as you do others, but not more or less than.

It is a good idea to help clients draw the line between "helpful" behavior, that is, being supportive or encouraging of others and "care-taking" or "rescuing" behavior, whereby one person rescues or steps in to do things for someone that the other person could do for him- or herself.

Codependency breeds insecurity. At some level, the helper implies that the individual being "helped" is weak or helpless, that is, not capable of taking care of him- or herself.

A client newly in treatment got overinvolved in caretaking and trying to solve other people's problems. She had lived in a group home as a teen, so she wanted to "help" teens with problems. Newly in recovery, she gave advice to others about their drug use. And while "helping" others, she neglected work on her own recovery, her interpersonal boundaries, and her *addiction* to a long-term, conflicted relationship.

When working with codependent clients, the best thing we can do is help them validate their own needs.

ENOUGH IS ENOUGH

Samantha Sheep heard a loud voice calling from across the pasture. It was her friend Pig. "Black sheep, black sheep, have you any wool?" Samantha called back, in an annoyed voice, "Go away and leave me alone!" She sounded very upset.

"Now wait a minute," you say. I suspect that you know the next line of this nursery rhyme is not supposed to be, "Go away and leave me alone." The next line is supposed to be, "Yes sir, yes sir, three bags full." So you might ask, "What is going on with Samantha Sheep?" And I might answer, "Sit down and relax, and I'll tell you."

Samantha was a sweet, kind, and generous sheep. She almost never talked to anyone in an annoyed voice. She had a big heart and gave freely of herself, even the wool off her back. She liked to do things to please others and make them happy. But this day, Samantha had a reason to be upset. She was naked and cold, and her breath came out like a foggy cloud as it hit the chilly air.

You might wonder why Samantha Sheep was naked and shivering in the cold on a sunny spring day. After all, a sheep is an animal that usually has plenty of soft, warm wool on its back.

Poor Samantha. She was too kind for her own good. On Monday, her friend Barn Cat came to see her and meowed, "Black sheep, black sheep, have you any wool?"

Samantha smiled and replied, "Yes cat, yes cat, three bags full."

"Oh, good!" said Barn Cat. "I want to make a lovely black wool hat to warm my ears when I sleep in the barn on cold spring nights."

Then Samantha sheared some wool off her back to give to Barn Cat so that she could make her hat. In case you did not know, "sheared" is a word that means to cut off the sheep's wool. It doesn't hurt when a sheep is sheared. The wool covering the sheep's body is clipped off (a little like a haircut), and later it grows back.

"Thank you for the wool!" purred Barn Cat as she ran back to the barn, twitching her tail. "You are a kind and generous friend."

That night, Samantha felt the cold wind blowing on her bare back and was glad she still had the rest of her wool to keep her warm. "It's good to share my wool," she thought. "I am a little chilly tonight, but my wool will grow back soon."

On Tuesday, her friend Watch Dog came to see her and barked, "Black sheep, black sheep, have you any wool?"

Samantha smiled and replied, "Yes dog, yes dog, three bags full."

"Oh good," said Watch Dog. "I want to make a black wool sweater to warm my back in the cold spring air."

Then Samantha sheared off the rest of the wool on her back, which was enough wool to make the dog's sweater.

"Thank you so much," barked Watch Dog as he ran off to protect the farm. "You are a kind and generous friend."

That night, the cold wind numbed Samantha's totally bare back. She curled up next to another sheep in the pasture to keep warm. Her teeth were chattering and she shivered all night.

Samantha thought, "I'm very cold tonight, but I don't want to complain. It is good to share my wool with others. My wool will grow back soon."

On Wednesday, her friend Milk Cow came to see Samantha and mooed, "Black sheep, black sheep, have you any wool?"

Samantha bleated, "Yes cow, yes cow, three bags full."

"Oh, good!" said Milk Cow. "I would like to make a long, black wool scarf to wear around my neck. It would look lovely with my black and white spots, and it will warm my neck on cold spring nights."

"You will look lovely wearing a long black scarf," agreed Samantha. Then Samantha sheared the wool off her belly, head, and rump so that Milk Cow could have her scarf.

Milk Cow said, "You are a kind and generous friend!" as she waddled back to the barn.

That night Samantha bleated in distress. She was totally naked and had nothing to keep her warm in the cold spring air.

"I hope I don't freeze to death," thought Samantha as a tear fell from her eye. "I have no more wool on my body. I know it will grow back in time, but that thought will not help me on this cold, spring night."

Poor Samantha did not sleep at all that night as she huddled with the other sheep in the pasture.

So now you understand why Samantha spoke to Pig in an annoyed voice the next morning when he came to ask her for some wool. But the minute Samantha said, "Go away and leave me alone!" she felt a little guilty. She really liked to be generous and give the wool off her back to her friends. She enjoyed pleasing them and making them happy. Samantha felt sad that she had nothing left to give.

And then her friend Pig did something that surprised Samantha. Pig walked over to her in the pasture and said kindly, "Why are you standing naked in the cold spring air? What has happened to all your wool?"

Samantha replied, "I gave my friends all the wool off my back. I like to please them and make them happy."

Pig said, "Enough is enough! It's wonderful to have friends and to do things to make them happy, but you need to keep some of your wool for yourself. You won't be much help to your friends if you end up frozen like a block of ice!"

He added, "Sometimes you have to take care of yourself before you take care of others."

Pig gave a loud, "OINK" that could be heard all the way to the barn, and he shouted, "Barn Cat, Watch Dog, and Milk Cow, please come out to the pasture."

Out of the barn came the cat, the dog, and the cow. Barn Cat was purring and wearing a lovely black wool hat. Watch Dog was panting happily, sporting a handsome black wool sweater. And Milk Cow gave a loud "Moo" as she showed off her long, black wool scarf. They wondered why Pig had called them out of the barn. They were afraid he might be charging them a fine for leaving such a "smelly mess" on the barnyard floor—Pig was the newly elected president of the Barnyard Association.

Then they saw their shivering friend Samantha standing in the pasture with Pig, and all three came running over.

"Samantha," meowed Barn Cat, "you are naked and have nothing to warm your head. You must borrow my wool hat!" And with that, Barn Cat put the hat on Samantha's head.

"Samantha," barked Watch Dog, "your back is bare and the air is cold. You must borrow my sweater." And with that, Watch Dog draped his new sweater over Samantha's shivering back.

Milk Cow mooed, "Samantha, you must borrow my scarf. It will warm your neck when the cold spring wind is blowing." And with that, Milk Cow wrapped her long, black scarf around Samantha's sheared neck.

"We're sorry," said Samantha's friends. "We didn't realize that you gave us all the wool off your back, neck, head, and belly. Please wear the hat, sweater, and scarf until your wool grows back."

Samantha smiled at her friends. "You are such good friends," she bleated. "Soon, my wool will grow back, and then I will return the hat, the sweater, and the scarf. Next time I'll keep a little wool for myself."

Samantha's friends headed back to the barn to clean up the "dirty mess" to avoid getting a fine. They drew straws to see which one would get the "dirtiest job" of bagging the "shit."

From that day forward, Samantha took good care of herself. She was still a kind and generous sheep, but after all, no one is expected to give ALL the wool off his or her back.

THE BOTTOM LINE: Enough is Enough!

FOOD FOR THOUGHT QUESTIONS

1. How are you like Samantha?
2. Which animal in the barnyard do you most identify with?
3. Are you more of a giver or a taker?
4. In what area of your life do you most need to say, "No!"?
5. What are three things you could do to take better care of yourself?

21

What Comes Next?

Planning Ahead

We have to each ask ourselves, "What is my gold?" Like the man in the next story, once we know what we are trying to find, we need to figure out where we need to go to find it. At times, the best choice is to move in a new direction. But we all get comfortable in our surroundings and change can be unsettling, especially when the known benefits of the current situation seem to outweigh the unknown benefits of making a change.

When someone is in the Contemplation Phase of the Stages of Change, he or she needs to weigh risks and benefits of the potential change. Motivational Interviewing is an excellent way to help a client be aware of the choices that are available. In Motivational Interviewing, there is often a "shit or get off the pot" moment, when the person must "make the move already!" or stop complaining.

A woman "stuck" in an unhappy marriage had neglected her needs for years. She had given up hobbies and interests for the "sake of" her husband, lived in a house she hated, and resented her partner's marijuana use. We read the story that follows and finished the session with guided imagery. Her assignment was to figure out an answer to the following question: "What is your gold?" Interestingly enough, when she came back in two weeks, she had already picked up an old hobby and gone house-hunting, empowered by the story's imagery.

The following story can be quite powerful in seeding the possibility of change and helping a client move toward Action.

GOLD IN THE DESERT

Once upon a time, a girl was taking a walk in the desert, just down the road from her house. Have you ever seen a desert? A desert is dry, bare, and flat as far as the eye can see. The hot sun glared down from high in the sky. Everything was dusty, and fine grains of sand kept getting into the girl's shoes. The heat made waves in the hazy, hot air, and off in the distance you could see the faint outline of a range of tall, snow-topped mountains. No one lived near the girl—her house was "out in the middle of nowhere" according to her friends.

As the girl walked, she took a drink from her water bottle and put some more sunscreen on her face and arms. Then suddenly the girl heard a loud voice: "Oh, CRAP!" The voice came from a tall man who was kneeling in the sand a few feet in front of her. Sweat was pouring down his red face as he scooped up some sand and sifted through it with a flat pan. The pan had very tiny holes in it and sand poured through them.

As the girl watched, the man threw down his sifter and said, again, very loudly, "Oh, CRAP!!!" The girl giggled to herself. Everyone knew that "CRAP" was a BAD WORD and not a nice thing to say. "I must be doing something wrong," said the red-faced man.

The girl was very curious and could not figure out what the man was doing. "Excuse me, Mister," the girl said as she approached, "What are you trying to do?"

"That's obvious," he said. "I want to be a miner, and I'm searching for gold. I've sifted sand all day and haven't found ANY gold. I'm starting to get very upset. I've always been told that if you believe in yourself and work hard, you will be successful."

The girl thought, "He is one strange man! Everyone knows you sift for gold in a stream or mine gold up in the mountains. There is no water here, and the mountains are miles away."

The girl said, "I can tell that you have been working hard—your face is all red and you are covered in sand!"

Then the man said, "I feel like a failure, because I haven't found any gold. I must be doing something wrong."

The girl replied, trying to not hurt his feelings, "Mister, you're not doing anything wrong, but there is no gold here. Never has been—never will be. You might find gold up in the mountains. You're using the right tools—you're just looking in the wrong place."

"What do you mean?" asked the man.

"You could use that pan to sift through the sand in a stream up near the mountains," the girl answered. "If you want to find gold, you need to leave the desert."

"Oh darn," he replied. "I was afraid of that. I've always lived in the desert and don't really want to go anywhere else. I want to stay in the desert AND find gold."

"Mister," said the girl, "if you stay here, you're never going to find gold."

The man protested, "But what if I try my hardest, and pray night and day, and use my very best sifting technique?"

The girl said, "You're fooling yourself if you expect to find gold in the desert. There will never be any gold here. Even if you try your hardest, pray night and day, and use your very best sifting technique, you won't succeed."

"But as I told you before," replied the man, "I don't want to go anywhere else. I don't like to travel, and I'm very comfortable in the desert."

The girl said, "Sifting for gold in the desert is like trying to squeeze water out of a rock."

"You can't squeeze water out of a rock!" the man said.

The girl smiled playfully and handed him a small, hard, dry desert rock. "Go ahead and try," she said. "Squeeze it really hard." Just for fun, he gave the rock a squeeze. Of course, nothing came out of the rock.

She said, "Squeeze a little harder." So the man squeezed with all his might, but no water came out.

The girl teased, "Maybe you're not doing it right. Maybe you need to twist it or sit on it or rub it—surely if you keep trying, you will squeeze some water out of that rock?"

The man replied, "No, I can't squeeze water out of this rock."

"And why is that?" the girl asked.

He stated, "Because there is no water in it."

"Exactly," said the girl, "and there is no gold in that sand. Go to where the gold is if you want to find the gold."

The man realized that the girl was very wise for her young years. He could stay where he was (and quit hoping to find gold) or move on to a new place where gold was plentiful (the word "plentiful" means LOTS of gold). Just *knowing* he had a choice made a difference.

THE BOTTOM LINE: Go for the gold!

FOOD FOR THOUGHT QUESTIONS

1. What is your gold?
2. What steps would you need to take (even if you think you can't) to find your gold?
3. What keeps you from moving in a new direction?
4. Even if you believe it is not possible, what would you most like to be doing five years from now?

22

Recognizing Danger

Women that have been hurt or abused in their relationships may return to those relationships somehow expecting or hoping for something to change. It is a Cinderella wish, a story full of fairy-tale magic where the girl gets the prince and everyone lives happily ever after. The hope remains that this time, things will be different—the pumpkin will become a coach and the magic will prevail!

Unfortunately, in the case of relational violence, the prince is often an ogre in disguise—and he's not a nice ogre like Shrek! The ogre inside the prince is cruel, mean, and controlling. He knows just how to play her; and he can turn on the tears and beg her forgiveness "just right." He has one goal—to change her mind and win her back.

The woman thinks, "He loves me—he's sorry—he sees what he did wrong and promises to change. I love him—I believe him. He must be my prince! No one this nice and sincere could really be an ogre!" One client told her therapist, "He's not so bad—he's really sorry he slapped me, and he has promised to treat me better."

The perpetrator prince promises to change and is often able to woo her lovingly back after an episode of abuse; but you can't trust someone with malevolent or controlling intentions. Promises to change during the honeymoon phase of the cycle of abuse are appealing, and it's OK to hope, but enduring behavior is the only good indicator of true change.

The only way the woman will see enduring behavior change in her partner is if she refuses to take him back until he works on his own issues.

Until a partner moves beyond lip-service change to actual behavior change, a woman is wise to keep some distance between herself and the partner that has harmed her.

THE HUNGRY ALLIGATOR AND THE MEAN SNAKE

A group of friends were walking through the muck of a Florida swamp one sunny day in June when they heard a most horrific sound. "HSSSSSS," was the sound. Do you know what makes that sound? I hate to say it was not a teakettle boiling on the stove. "HSSSSS," came the sound again. Slithering their way was an ugly, mean-looking, bright green snake with a huge mouth and two big fangs sticking out of his mouth like a pair of buckteeth. With him was a nasty-looking, bumpy-snouted, long-tailed alligator.

"Hello, neighborssssssssss," hissed the snake with a sly smile, when he was about 20 feet away.

Kanga Kangaroo called out to her small friends, Madeleine Monkey and Mike Manatee, "Oh me, oh my, I don't have room for the two of you inside my pouch. Quick, get behind me!" You may be surprised to hear that a kangaroo, monkey, and manatee were hanging out together in a Florida swamp. Well, Kanga and Madeleine had escaped for the afternoon from a nearby zoo, and their friend Mike lived in a small cove in Smerna Beach. Kanga had a baby kangaroo in her pouch, which was why she had no room for Madeleine or Mike at the present time!

"I'm in a bad mood," said the alligator.

"Me, too!" said the snake. "Let's go eat someone," he said.

"Yeah," said the alligator. "I feel like eating someone, too. I haven't had anything to eat for two weeks! And if I don't find anyone delectable enough to eat," he sneered, "I'm going to at least bite someone with my big, sharp teeth."

"Yessss!" hissed the snake. "I'd love to coil up and strike someone with my fangs." In case you do not know it, the word "delectable" means something very tasty or delicious.

Both the alligator and snake were in snappy, mean, sourpuss moods. It might have been because the snake had almost been turned into a snakeskin purse the week before; and the alligator had almost become someone's expensive alligator shoes. They had escaped with their lives in the nick of time when hunters had chased them through the Everglades, a large swamp in Florida.

The alligator and snake were also more hungry than usual. As the alligator had said, it had been two weeks since they had anything to eat. Because of the drought and the population explosion in Florida, there was not much food to be had for snakes and alligators. A drought is a long dry spell without rain; and a population explosion is when there are too many animals or people around and it is too crowded. Florida is definitely one place that is much too crowded, especially with alligators, snakes, and older retired people.

"Hello," said Kanga bravely to the snake and the alligator as they approached. "Don't come any closer," she said.

"Lunch," said the snake to the alligator in a quiet sneaky voice.

"Oh, goodie," said the alligator, licking his chops and creeping a few steps closer.

"No," said Kanga. "Please move back. It's not nice to eat your neighbors."

Kanga had been wise to put her young friends behind her and to ask the alligator and snake to move back. She knew that you should never let an alligator or a snake get too close. It is their nature to strike, even if they act nice, smile, and pretend to be your friend. You would be very foolish indeed to let an alligator or snake give you a hug or kiss. If you let a boa constrictor curl up around you, he might squeeze the life out of you before you even realized what was happening. If you let an alligator give you a backrub, he could take a bite out of you from behind and you would never see it coming. And you would be even more foolish to accept an invitation to go swimming with them or to meet them for dinner. Probably, you would *be* the dinner if you accepted *that* invitation.

Kanga whispered to Mike and Madeleine, "They haven't eaten in two weeks, so I think they are going to eat *us* if we don't get them some food! Why don't Madeleine and I go back to the zoo to get some food for them and bring it back?"

Madeleine whispered back, "Yes, let's get some food for them to eat. Then they won't eat *us*. Alligators and snakes are much more agreeable when they are full. They are downright mean when they are hungry!"

Kanga told the alligator and snake, "We don't really know what it feels like to be hungry. They feed us every day at the zoo, and we are well taken care of. Mike over there gets plenty of plants off the bottom of the cove. Why don't you let us go back to the zoo for some food for the two of you? Then you can eat until you are totally full."

"Alright," said snake and alligator. "We'll wait here with your friend Mike Manatee while you go get us some food, and if you're not back in fifteen minutes, we'll eat your friend." That was a horrible thought for Kanga and Madeleine. They knew that manatees are large, gentle animals that move quite slowly. Mike had no protection against the awful, hungry alligator and mean snake.

Madeleine and Kanga went quickly back to the zoo and begged for some food to give the alligator and the snake. Luckily, it was the end of the day, and the zoo snack bars had quite a bit of uneaten, leftover food. They collected the biggest pile of food that you have ever seen and returned to where the alligator and snake waited with Mike Manatee. Madeleine was pushing a wheelbarrow full of food, and Kanga's pouch overflowed with the bounty.

"Open your mouths," said Kanga. Each opened wide. The snake could only open the front of his mouth at his hinged jaw, but the alligator's open mouth was huge and long, with many sharp teeth. "You need to use more toothpaste," said Kanga to the alligator, "as even from 20 feet away, I can see that your teeth are quite yellow."

The alligator snapped at her with annoyance and she hopped back another step. Kanga said, "I hope you'll be in a better mood after you have something to eat."

So Madeleine and Kanga began throwing them food. They used a slingshot to propel the food 25 feet, to keep the alligator and snake at a safe distance.

First, Madeleine tossed them five hamburgers, eight slushies, and three bags of popcorn. Next, six hotdogs, three chicken nuggets, two ice cream bars and seven snow cones from the snack bar flew their way.

"Snap!" went the alligator's mouth.

"Yesssss!" said the snake. Soon all the food had disappeared.

"We're still hungry!" shouted the snake and alligator. "Give us more food, or we're going to eat your friend!"

"OK," said Kanga. She reached inside her pouch and pulled out ten bags of salted peanuts, two servings of nachos with peppers, ten cheeseburgers, and five ice cream cones. After a mighty pull on the slingshot, Kanga let go and slung the last of the food to the alligator and snake.

The not-quite-as-hungry alligator and snake gobbled it all down. As the last cheeseburger and ice cream cone disappeared, two loud burps sounded: "URRPPPP!" "URRPPPP!"

"Please say excuse me," said Kanga sternly, "and then say thank you!"

The now quite agreeable alligator and snake each said "Excuse me!" and "Thank you" as they reported that they were quite full. They were so full that they returned to the Everglades swamp to take a long afternoon nap and did not try to eat Mike Manatee or his friends.

Kanga and Madeleine said goodbye to Mike and went back to the zoo to eat lunch and take a long nap. Sometimes you need to take a nap after such a scary adventure.

You may find this story helpful the next time you come across a hungry alligator or a mean snake. First, get help right away and do whatever you need to do to remain safe. You might try feeding them, from 25 feet away, in case they are very hungry. But if that does not work, I recommend that you offer them a safe place to stay, like a cage or zoo! For when an alligator says to a snake, "Let's have our friends over for dinner" he means exactly that!

THE BOTTOM LINE: Do what you need to do to stay safe!

FOOD FOR THOUGHT QUESTIONS

1. Why should you not trust the alligator?
2. Can alligators change? If so, what would it take?
3. What has to be in place for someone to be safe with an alligator?
4. In your life, what would need to be in place for you (and your children) to be safe?
5. Has an *alligator* ever persuaded you to trust him? What was the result?

23

Opening Your Heart

The metaphor in the following story was provided by a 16-year-old girl whose mother had broken her heart over and over again. When asked what was going on when she acted "mean" and rejecting toward others, she said, with a smile, "I have a plastic heart. I sent my real heart away on vacation. That's why I'm so hard-hearted!" The girl had difficulty trusting others and automatically pushed them away when they got too close or when she judged that they did not *really* care about her.

A woman's heart can easily grow numb or closed after repeated rejection, hurt, and betrayal. After awhile, her heart can feel empty, and it becomes hard to trust again. A woman who has been abused throughout life may be cautious about beginning any close relationships.

Through treatment, "the girl with the plastic heart" realized that she could love and be loved; but she also learned that she could not expect or hope for her mother to change. Most women involved in relational violence will relate to the main character's pain and find it easier to talk about the ways in which their hearts have been broken.

THE GIRL WITH THE PLASTIC HEART (Dedicated to "P")

A teenage girl and her friend were walking down the sidewalk on a bright sunny day. As they approached an older woman, the woman smiled and said, "Hi, how are you today?" and stepped aside to let the girls pass.

The girl smirked at her friend as if to say, "Just watch what I'm going to do!" She frowned at the woman and said in a rude voice, "What's it to you? Go away and mind your own business old lady."

As if that wasn't enough, she deliberately bumped the startled woman hard enough to knock her off balance. The woman had to step off the sidewalk into the muddy grass to avoid falling.

The girl's friend helped the woman back onto the sidewalk as her friend walked briskly ahead. She explained, "Don't mind her. She knocks *everyone* off balance."

"And why is that?" asked the woman.

The friend replied, "It's because she has a plastic heart."

"A plastic heart?" the woman asked.

"Yes," replied the girl's friend. "Her real heart is on vacation."

"Why did her heart go on vacation?" the woman asked.

"Well," said the friend, "Her real heart got broken over and over by those she loved—especially by her mother. It needed a rest and time to heal."

"When someone breaks your heart," said the woman, "You need to find love somewhere else, to help your heart heal."

The friend replied sadly, "A heart that gets broken many times takes longer and longer to heal. My friend's real heart was becoming scarred from all the hurt and sadness. So she replaced it with a plastic heart. A plastic heart has no feeling—that's why she says or does whatever she pleases."

"Was sending her heart on vacation her only choice?" asked the woman.

The friend replied, "The doctor wanted her to keep her real heart and take better care of it. Her friends suggested she avoid people that had broken her heart. But my friend is very stubborn. She thinks she knows what's best for her."

The woman's face grew concerned. "Hearts on vacation grow lazy, and it's hard to convince them to come home. Let's go talk to your friend."

The woman and the girl's friend ran to catch up with the girl with the plastic heart.

"What do *you* want?" the girl asked her friend. "And why is that ugly old woman with you?"

The friend replied, "I told her about your plastic heart."

"My plastic heart is none of her business," said the girl.

"That may be true," interrupted the woman. "But I have to tell you something."

The girl rolled her eyes and said, "OK, old woman, tell me—I'm sure it will be something stupid."

The woman spoke quickly. "Your heart belongs with you—not at a vacation resort. Hearts on vacation become lazy and selfish. Your real heart is probably complaining to everyone that you are a heartless person for sending it away and forgetting about it."

The girl frowned and looked annoyed. "I'm going to give my heart a piece of my mind!" she exclaimed. "Let's go!"

They all traveled to the tropical island resort where the real heart was staying. The woman had been right. The heart was sitting by the side of a pool, all flabby and lazy, wearing glittery sunglasses and sipping a fruity drink.

"Where have you been and what do you want?" the real heart asked the girl in an annoyed voice.

The girl decided it was time to end the heart's vacation. "Your vacation is over—it's time to go home and get back to work."

"You don't need *me*," said the heart. "You have that cheap plastic model."

"The plastic heart is brittle and cracked," said the girl.

"Well, I don't know if I *want* to come back," said the heart. "I could have helped you make friends or find real love. But nooooo, you had to replace me!" Then the heart took a really cheap shot. "You're no better than the people that broke *your* heart. You sent me away and forgot about me!"

"I'm not like the people that broke my heart!" said the girl. "I'm loyal and dependable, and I keep my promises. I care about others, even though I may not always show it."

She added, "I sent you away on vacation so that you could heal, and you have healed just fine. So pack your things. You're coming home with me." The heart realized it did not have a choice and went to pack.

While the real heart was packing, the woman came over and handed the girl a soft scarf. "Here," said the woman, "It's a heart-warmer, to protect your real heart from being broken. I want you to have it."

The real heart returned with her suitcase, ready to go home with the girl. The girl wrapped her real heart gently in the heart warmer and quickly replaced the plastic heart.

"There," she said. "That's better."

Inside the girl, the real heart whispered something to her that no one else could hear.

"I almost forgot," the girl said as she spoke to the woman. "Thanks for the heart-warmer. I'm sorry I was so hard-hearted before!"

"That's OK," said the woman. "I understand."

The woman said goodbye to the girl and her friend. She saw a visible difference in the girl now that her real heart was back in place. She knew that the heart-warmer would protect the girl from hurt.

Later, the girl wondered what had happened to the brittle plastic heart with all the cracks in it. The girl would never know it, but the woman had spoken the truth when she said, "I understand."

Believe it or not, the girl's plastic heart was sitting on a shelf in the old woman's house. It sat right next to a second cracked plastic heart and a photo of the woman's real heart lazing away at a tropical resort.

THE BOTTOM LINE: Don't set your heart aside!

FOOD FOR THOUGHT QUESTIONS

1. How are you like the girl?
2. Describe something one of your parents did to break your heart.
3. Discuss how you react when your heart is broken.
4. Have you ever put your heart aside? What do you need to do to bring it back?

24

Expecting the Worst

Fight or Flight

An unfortunate outcome of domestic violence is that the victim has been told many things about others that aren't true but that she comes to believe: "Don't trust others!" "Don't let anyone get too close—they will hurt you." "I'm the only one that understands you." "Others only tell you what you want to hear." "I'm the only one you can trust!"

The DV perpetrator sets up conditions of isolation and fear so that the woman will not turn to others for help. It is like an insurance policy that breeds mistrust of others and keeps the victim dependent on the perpetrator. Sooner or later the woman expects the worst from those around her.

When someone expects the worst, she acts in ways that reinforce her beliefs. When someone goes looking for betrayal, he or she finds it; if she expects to be hurt and pulls away, she is likely to experience rejection. It is a vicious cycle, one negative life event after another.

Intervention needs to interrupt the cycle of mistrust; since even in a new, healthier, more positive environment a woman with negative expectations may be unable to notice small steps toward success. The story that follows describes the cognitive and emotional challenges that confront those that expect the worst.

LOOKING FOR LAND MINES IN DISNEYLAND

The little girl had just walked through the Disneyland front gate to spend a fun day at the park with her family. I know it is not nice to stare, but she simply could not help it. *You* might think she was staring at Cinderella, who was walking toward the castle ahead. Or maybe at Goofy and Donald Duck who were doing a little dance to entertain the children.

No, she was staring at a Marine, a female soldier in full combat uniform. The soldier was moving forward slowly, one step at a time, tapping her foot on each square stone of the path that lay before her. She had on dark sunglasses and was frowning with intense concentration. Her gun was drawn, her face was sweating, and she was crouched over as if ready to run at a moment's notice.

The little girl could not resist running over to the soldier and tugging on her sleeve. "Excuse me!" she said. "Do you mind me asking what you are doing?"

The Marine had not noticed the girl approaching—when she felt the tug on her sleeve, she was startled, and instinctively turned her gun on the little girl.

"Hey!" said the little girl. "I'm not the enemy—you can put the gun down and answer my question."

The Marine replied, "Sorry about that. I'm looking for land mines!"

"In Disneyland?" asked the girl.

"AB-SO-LUTE-LY!" declared the Marine. "You never know when you might run into a land mine and get blown to bits—even in Disneyland. I know. I was deployed in the Middle East last year and every time I turned around someone was stepping on a land mine. I stepped on one myself and narrowly escaped death. Others were not so lucky."

"Everyone knows that there are no land mines in Disneyland," the little girl said to the Marine.

"You never know," said the Marine. "And I don't want anything to blow up in my face! It's better to be safe than sorry."

The girl was silent. She didn't know what to say. The Marine was missing out on the fun of Disneyland because she did not feel safe.

The girl suggested, "If you would put away the gun, take off the body armor and go on a few rides with me, maybe you could relax and realize that you *are* safe here. Disneyland is not the Middle East—there aren't any land mines in Disneyland. The Middle East was a dangerous place and bad things happened to you there. But that was then, and this is now."

The soldier would not agree to leave the gun but took off the body armor. As she walked with the girl to the Dumbo ride, she continued to tap her foot on the walkway, by habit looking for land mines.

When they were almost at the line for the ride, a large costumed Mickey Mouse figure approached, holding out his white-gloved hand.

The soldier crouched, pointed her gun at Mickey and shouted, "Stop right there, Mouse! Take off those gloves and show me your hands!"

Poor Mickey. He had never had a gun pointed at him at Disneyland. Mickey started to shake with fear. And all the little children around Mickey Mouse started to cry.

"What's going on?" Mickey squeaked in a high voice.

"I just know you have a hand grenade hidden in those huge white gloves!" said the Marine.

"I only wanted to shake your hand and thank you for serving our country," squeaked Mickey.

Mickey tossed both white gloves on the ground and showed his hands, nothing in either of them, and the Marine lowered her gun.

"Sorry," muttered the Marine. "Guess I was mistaken. When I was in the Middle East, our tank took a hit from a grenade that was hidden inside someone's shirt. You never know when something might blow up in your face—better to be safe than sorry!"

The little girl answered in a stern voice. "Well, you're not in the Middle East anymore. You're in Disneyland. That was then and this is now. There aren't any land mines or hand grenades in Disneyland. No one here is your enemy. It's time to stop accusing people of trying to hurt you, and get over the past. You're scaring all the children!"

The Marine agreed to lock her gun up at the Disneyland office, since she didn't want to accidentally shoot someone like Mickey Mouse. She got in line with the little girl and rode the Dumbo ride. She felt pretty good, even without her armor and gun. Next, they decided to ride It's a Small World After All—it was really cute, but I have to tell you that the singing of the cheerful, little dolls really started to get on her nerves by the time the boat reached the end of the ride.

When the park was getting ready to close, the Marine collected her gun and body armor. She had bought a Cinderella T-shirt to wear over her uniform and was much more relaxed than she had been earlier that day. She thanked the little girl for showing her around and giving her good advice.

As the soldier walked out the exit, she turned around one last time and said to the girl, "It's hard to break old habits, but I'm going to try to stop looking for land mines in Disneyland. I have two more days left on my three-day pass, and if I want to get the most out of my Disneyland experience, I need to keep telling myself, "Then is not now!"

The girl agreed. "Yes, there is a time to protect yourself from danger and a time to relax and understand that the danger has passed. Maybe in time you'll find the wisdom to know the difference."

THE BOTTOM LINE: Then is not now!

FOOD FOR THOUGHT QUESTIONS

1. How are you like the soldier in Disneyland?
2. What happened to you in the past that made you not trust others?
3. What are your land mines?
4. What does the soldier need to do to get more comfortable in Disneyland?

Part IV

STORIES FOR ACTION

This six-month phase of active change is one where clients consciously choose new behaviors, accept feedback and support, and put into practice the plan that was developed during the Preparation Phase. Women in the Action Phase are ready to face obstacles and challenges, and they show insight into their previous behavior.

It is a delight to work with clients in this phase of treatment, as they are full of enthusiasm and motivation. Only a small subgroup of women in treatment are actually in this phase, as it is a brief six-month period of change; and most effort goes into Pre-Contemplation, Contemplation, Preparation, and Maintenance.

What seems crucial during this phase is that the changes become attributed to the client's own efforts and are well cemented, that is, hardened up and resilient to stressors. If the changes last for six months, the Stages of Change model assumes that they will last, however, there are different degrees of change. It is important during this phase to remind the client of where she started—to help her see that she got where she is through *her own efforts*, not luck, magic, or the therapist's skill. The client needs to attribute the changes to her own intelligence, motivation, and hard work. In addition, the client needs to understand that it will take continued focus and hard work to maintain the changes.

The stories in this section are for the phase of active change—they will propel trauma-focused intervention, mood management, addressing addictive behaviors, and attachment issues.

25

Understanding PTSD

The symptoms of PTSD are many and diverse, leaving victims of complex or severe relational trauma confused about what they are going through. They may feel "crazy" or "different" than those around them, resulting in them avoiding social interaction. They may sleep long hours yet be constantly exhausted; or have trouble sleeping due to nightmares and anxiety. Many persons with PTSD experience high autonomic arousal (agitation, strong startle, hypervigilance) yet others shut down and feel emotionally numb. Some abuse victims develop gastrointestinal symptoms, headaches, or auto-immune disorders (McCollum, 2006). It is common for those with PTSD to be short-tempered and irritable with those around them. Most persons with undiagnosed PTSD avoid cues that remind them of the abuse.

One client did not realize her symptoms were related to prior abuse. She could not sleep at night, she carried a pocketknife for protection, and she did not feel comfortable out in public. For years she had been battered and demeaned by men; and her current husband threatened her and her children.

The story that follows was written to describe the symptoms of and healing from PTSD. It may be used in group sessions or individual treatment. Individuals will relate to different characters in the story and some will find themselves identifying with both the victim and the perpetrator. The story has the capacity to trigger memories of childhood abuse and also reminds adults of the patience and empathy needed to help children recover from traumatic events.

LUCKY THE JUNKYARD DOG

One upon a time there was a two-year-old dog named Lucky. He lived with his three much younger brothers and sisters in a dark alley behind the local pool hall. Lucky's mother had been homeless when he was born and she had trouble feeding her large family. She ran around a lot with her friends and there was never enough food to go around. Sometimes when her puppies were being normal young, active dogs she barked, "You F*#$in Brats, be quiet. You're getting on my last nerve and I need some peace and quiet!" When she got mean like that, the puppies put their tails between their legs and scurried off.

Lucky tried to be a good big brother. He loved his brothers and sisters and tried to protect them at any cost. He let the puppies cuddle around him at night to stay warm, he went hunting for food every night, and he growled at anyone that came too close.

Lucky dreamed of living in a home with a fireplace, a soft bed, a kind master, and a big grassy yard. One day a big man came into the alley and said, "Hey Joe, there's those wild dogs I talked about. That big one there would make a good guard dog for the junkyard." Before Lucky could growl or run off, the man kicked him hard in the side. Lucky yelped in pain and tried to nip the man in self-defense. The man tossed a rope around his neck, threw him into the back of a red pickup truck, and drove off to the junkyard.

Three years later, Lucky was still living the life of a junkyard dog. The mean junkyard manager kept Lucky on a heavy chain and thought it was funny to tease and torment him. He sometimes held out a juicy steak bone—and when the hungry dog went for it, the man kicked him in the side and pulled it away with a laugh. Lucky could never tell when the man might pet him or when he might curse at him in a loud mean voice and slap him in the head.

The junkyard manager had a wife who was nice to Lucky. But the man hit her too and cursed at her in a loud mean voice. When the man came near her in anger, Lucky tried to protect her by growling and stood between her and the man. She usually pushed Lucky behind her, to keep him safe.

Lucky hated the loud, mean voice and the hitting. He hated hearing the woman shout at the man to get away and really hated hearing her cry when she was hurt.

"You're a good dog, Lucky," the woman said. "Don't you mind him." But Lucky did mind, and he didn't feel like a good dog. He thought there must be something he could do to keep her safe, but he just couldn't figure it out.

Lucky never knew when the man might hurt him. When he heard the man coming, he slunk into the corner with his tail between his legs and growled. When Lucky heard the man shout or curse, he whimpered and stuck his nose between his front paws. He never felt safe and sometimes wished he had never been born. He couldn't protect the woman and he couldn't escape.

One day, the junkyard gate opened and a big four-wheel-drive pulled in with a load of scrap metal. The junkyard manager had gone to the restroom, so Lucky was alone. "Hey, good buddy," said the man who was unloading his truck. Lucky growled and backed away. The man came a little closer and sounded concerned. "Where did you get all those cuts and bruises, little guy? Your ribs are showing—are you hungry? I have a leftover burger in my truck—would you like it?"

The man went back to his truck to get another load of junk and brought a McDonald's bag with him. "Here you go," he said as he tossed Lucky the burger. Lucky lunged at the treat and gobbled it down. "You're half-starved," said the man. "No one should treat a dog like this."

When the mean junkyard manager came back outside, Lucky growled and slunk away with his tail between his legs. The man raised his leg to kick Lucky, and the nice man said, "Cut that out! You've been beating that dog and he's half-starved. What you're doing is against the law. You're going to let me take that dog with me or I'm going to call the authorities. So what is it? The dog goes with me or I make that call?"

The junkyard man already had a court record, so he unchained Lucky and put him in the man's truck. "You'll be sorry, Mister," he said with a sneer. "This mutt ain't going to be no housedog—he has no love in him, just meanness."

"We'll see about that," said the nice man as he drove off.

The man drove Lucky to his new home—a nice ranch with a fireplace and a big grassy yard. Lucky ran inside when the man opened the door but headed down to the lower level and slunk into a dark corner. When the man came near him, he growled. The man spoke in a soft, quiet voice, but any minute Lucky expected him to shout, curse, or hit. When the man's wife came to meet Lucky, he wagged his tail a little and stood between her and her husband, baring his teeth.

"That poor dog," said the man's wife. "Let's give him some loving care and time to heal. Maybe he'll learn to trust us."

Lucky didn't trust them. Not even when they gave him a soft bed with a thick blanket. Not even when they fed him treats like steak and liver bits. Not even when they spoke in soft voices. Not even when he realized that his food and water dishes were never allowed to empty.

Finally after quite some time, Lucky realized that the man and woman were *really* nice. They weren't faking it, and they weren't going to hurt him. They gave him a red ball, and every day they took him outside to play. For Lucky, playing was like something from outer space! At first,

Lucky hid under the deck—he thought they might throw the ball **at** him. But one morning he figured out they wanted him to chase and pick it up when they threw it. When he ran after the ball, he heard them laugh and say, "Good boy!" He wagged his tail a little at their praise. Before long, Lucky could not get enough of the "fetch" game.

One day, the man held out a juicy steak bone. "Come here, boy," said the man. Lucky almost growled. Somewhere in his memory was another man holding a steak bone. "It's OK, Lucky. Come get the bone," said the man in a kind voice. Lucky moved, one slow step at a time, toward the nice man. He grabbed the bone in his mouth and ran away with it so that man couldn't hit him or take it back.

"That's the other man," thought Lucky, "but it's hard to forget."

Lucky began to let the man's wife pet him at night before bed. She stroked his scarred back and crooned, "You sweet dog. We are blessed to have you in our lives. We love you!" Lucky liked her gentle, firm touch, and he rolled over to let her pet his belly.

Lucky finally felt safe and loved. He took walks in the neighborhood with the kind master and his wife. He sometimes growled at other people when they came too close, but his master said, "It's OK, Lucky, we won't let anyone hurt you."

One day on a walk, Lucky heard a very loud voice shouting, "You loser!—take your sorry butt back in the house." A very angry big man was raising his fist and shouting at his son. *Instantly,* Lucky's tail went between his legs and he started to growl. The loud voice scared him, and the cursing made him shiver and shake. Lucky pulled away, but his owner held him firmly by the leash.

"No Lucky, it's OK. Good Boy. Sit! Stay!" said his owner in a quiet firm voice as he reached down to pet him. "You still think something bad might happen to you, but never again. My wife and I will keep you safe. We love you." He stroked Lucky gently on the head and talked to him until he quit shaking.

Then Lucky's owner spoke just loudly enough for the other man to hear him. "That's no way to talk to anyone, and you scared my dog. If you're going to talk like that, take it inside." The angry man said, "F— you!" but he went in the house and closed the door.

Lucky's owner walked him back home, but Lucky still felt scared. He ran downstairs with his tail between his legs and slunk into the corner. He felt like growling at or biting his owner or the owner's wife. It made no sense, because they were so nice to him. But somewhere in his dog memory, he remembered a loud voice with kicks and hits, and he could almost taste the old pain and fear. He slept downstairs alone that night, ignoring his soft warm bed, and refusing to eat.

Luckily, it didn't take long for the man and his wife to help Lucky through that rough spot, like a bump in the road. Pretty soon he was back to sleeping in his bed and playing in the yard. There were a few more rough spots now and then, but his family was patient—they understood that bad memories last a long time. And every night, as they watched TV, ate popcorn, and fed Lucky dog treats, they said, "Lucky, you are a blessing in our lives!" And every night, right before bed, Lucky rolled over on his back, bared his belly and whined for just one more petting, please, as he thought, "This is as close to Heaven as it gets!"

THE BOTTOM LINE: Loving care helps but healing takes time!

FOOD FOR THOUGHT QUESTIONS

1. Who do you most identify with in the story?
2. How are you like the mean man?
3. How are you like Lucky?
4. How are you like the nice man?
5. If you were Lucky, what one thing did the man or his wife do that would help the most?
6. When you worry and can't sleep or feel like snapping at someone, what is going on for you?

26

Telling Your Story

Trauma Narratives

Going through treatment for relational trauma is quite painful—sort of a "no pain, no gain" process. It appears that in order to heal neurobiological pathways, an abuse victim needs to tell his or her story, decrease arousal to trauma cues, make sense of the traumatic events in one's life context, and learn new coping skills (Cozolino, 2006; Siegel & Hartzell, 2003). All of this takes energy, commitment, and courage. Quite a few clients drop out of treatment in order to avoid talking about what happened—some would rather "put it in the past" and pretend that it is "over." Unfortunately, these individuals too often continue to go through life with high stress/arousal and relational difficulties.

The story that follows was written to help a nine-year-old victim of complex trauma. She had drawn an elaborate picture of a brown bear that fell in a black pit and ended up black in color and badly injured. She pointed out that when someone fell in the pit, they could survive the first time, but if they fell a second time, they would die. She then drew red blobs in the pit, declaring, "Those are the hearts of the people that died in the pit." She had recently come to a group home from a string of abusive foster and adoptive homes. She told the therapist, "We have to help him be brown again!"

Women that live with the lingering pain of prior abuse yearn to "get back" to "normal." This child's story is a powerful representation of abuse and recovery. We have found the story to be helpful to those of all ages, in that it gives them a framework in which to describe the pain of being wounded inside and out. The story encourages victims of abuse to talk about what happened in their lives and provides hope.

A BEAR OF A DIFFERENT COLOR
(Dedicated to "K," whose own story brought Bear Bear to life)

Bear Bear, a small black bear, frowned. "I should be happy," Bear complained in a grouchy voice. "I should be happy to be out of the pit. But noooooo, I'm still not happy."

Bear's best friend, Brown Squirrel, scrambled down a nearby tree trunk and raced over to where Bear was complaining. Squirrel, with a large acorn in his mouth, asked, "Mwass wongh?"

Bear said, "Squirrel, with that acorn in your mouth, I can't understand what you're saying."

Squirrel smiled, spit out the acorn, and said, more clearly, "What's wrong?"

Bear replied, "I'm having bad dreams about falling in the black pit and I'm afraid to walk in the forest. I want my old life back—I used to be a happy, brown bear. I was born brown, and that's the way I liked it. Well, now I'm not brown and I'm not happy!"

The black pit that Bear was talking about was on the other side of the forest. You might be wondering how a little bear had happened to fall into such a pit. Well, as they say, "One thing leads to another."

It was just starting to get dark outside the afternoon Bear decided to take a walk in the forest. Bear didn't realize how late in the day it was. Then Bear found a honey tree and got a little distracted trying to get some honey out of the tree without being stung by bees.

Before Bear knew it, it was dark. In the darkness, Bear took the wrong path—the one that led to the pit.

"There are warning signs for the pit on that path," you say. "Ones that say 'Danger—do not go any further!' and 'Danger, deep black pit ahead!' Why didn't Bear see them and stop?"

Well, the pit's warning signs were too small, and Bear could not see them in the dark.

"But what about the guards?" you ask. "There are guards posted in front of the pit!"

That's true—there were two guards sitting in front of the pit, and they were supposed to stay awake and alert. But they had fallen asleep and could not warn Bear of the danger ahead.

Since Bear did not see the warning signs and the guards were asleep, you can imagine what happened. Yes, Bear fell into the deep, dark pit. When Bear hit the bottom of the pit, black, nasty, sticky, smelly goop splashed all around and covered Bear from head to toe. Bear survived the fall, but lay there for hours with a broken back.

"Please help me, somebody—anybody!" Bear cried out in pain for several long hours. Finally, a deer running through the woods heard Bear's cries and woke up the guards. That is how Bear got rescued from the pit and taken to the hospital.

The hospital fixed Bear's broken back, but no one could figure out how to wash off the black goop. The goop was an awful reminder of the fall, and Bear wanted to "come clean."

Squirrel wrinkled up his bushy brow and said, "Ah, so that's what's wrong, Bear. The fall into the pit changed you. You want to be brown again and you want to be happy. Let's go to the Recovery Center. It is a healing place. Maybe they can figure out how to help you."

It was a long walk to the Recovery Center. When they arrived, Squirrel said, "Go ahead Bear, just knock on the front door and tell them why we're here."

Bear knocked sharply on the broad wooden door. The door opened.

"May I help you?" asked a kind voice.

"Yes," said Bear. "My name is Bear Bear, and this is my friend Squirrel. I fell in the dangerous pit on the other side of the forest—the one where the guards sit day and night. I got covered with black, smelly goop. My friend thought that you might be able to help me."

"Hello, Bear and Squirrel," said the person. "Please come inside."

Bear and Squirrel stepped through the open door to enter the Recovery Center, which smelled really nice and looked a little like a health spa. As you walked in, you could hear the sounds of ocean waves. There were colorful flowers all around and healers of all types providing hugs, refreshments, and music.

"Look Squirrel!" said Bear in an excited voice. He pointed to a big hot tub in the middle of the room, one with purple bubbles bubbling on top. Next to the hot tub was a fountain with sweet-smelling green slime gurgling out of it. There was a pile of spa towels for when you got out of the hot tub, as soft as down blankets—and believe it or not, they even smelled like whipped cream!

Once they were inside, the person said, "I am a healer, and I know about that awful pit. Many children fall in when the guards are asleep. It is a terrible thing indeed. Sometimes, children are at the pit's edge before they realize where they are, and then it is too late. It's a good thing you survived, because many do not."

Bear told the healer, "I'm glad I survived, but I want to be brown again, more than anything else in the world."

The healer replied, "I can help you get rid of the black goop, but it's not an easy cure."

"Does the cure hurt?" asked Bear.

The healer answered, "Yes, but it is not as painful as falling in the pit. The healing takes a little time, so you can't be in a hurry. But I am a gentle healer, and I'll help you if that is what you want."

"Yes," said Bear and Squirrel at the same time. "Please help!"

The healer said, "To wash off the black goop, you must soak in the hot tub." So Bear stepped down into the hot tub with all the purple bubbles. It was very hot and burned Bear's sensitive skin, enough to make the little bear cry.

"I'm sorry, little bear," said the healer. "I know that the healing waters hurt at first."

Bear sat in the tub, and Squirrel sat right there next to Bear, offering his paw to hold. Bear said, "Thank you, Squirrel. I'm glad I don't have to go through this alone!"

"It's OK, Bear," said Squirrel. "You're worth it!"

The hot solution bubbled around Bear and soaked all the way deep-down through the black goop into Bear's skin. Little by little, it washed Bear clean. Then the healer helped Bear out of the tub, offered a soft towel, and provided a nice-smelling lotion for Bear's tender skin. Bear was now a lovely golden brown color.

"Can I look in a mirror?" asked Bear. The healer led Bear to a mirror. Bear stood still for a few minutes, looked in the mirror, and said, "I can see that the black goop is gone and I'm brown again. But I still don't feel happy. I don't want to complain, but the hot tub didn't fix that."

The healer said, "When you fell in the pit, you were so shocked and scared that you gulped in some of the black goop. Getting rid of the black goop on the outside doesn't get rid of the black goop on the inside."

"Inside me?" asked Bear with horror. "How can I get rid of something bad inside me that I can't even see?"

"You need to go through a second type of healing," the healer said.

"I'll do whatever you say," said Bear.

The healer told Bear, "For the second type of healing, you pick out a special healing potion and drink it. After you drink the potion, you tell your story. That's what makes the potion work."

"My story?" asked Bear.

"You know," said the healer, "the story of how you fell in the pit and what happened to you—how awful it is that the guards didn't keep you safe, and how you felt when you realized you were falling and might die; how you landed in the black, smelly goop and broke your back; and how scared you were when you thought you would never get out of there alive."

Bear argued, "I'll drink the potion, but I *won't* talk about the fall or the pit. I spend almost every waking moment trying not to think about falling in the pit. Talking about it would make it even worse."

"Well," said the healer in a gentle voice, "that's the only way to heal inside. As you tell your story, the potion dissolves the black goop. Once the healing is done, you'll stop having bad dreams and stop thinking about falling in the pit."

Bear thought hard about how much better life would be if the nasty, black goop was gone, outside and in and said, "OK, I'll drink the potion and talk about what happened to me. I don't really have a choice."

"You always have a choice," said the healer.

It was true. Bear had a choice. So Bear picked a potion that was all the colors of the rainbow and swallowed it down. It was warm and tasty, and it quickly spread all through Bear's body.

After Bear drank the potion, the healer said, "When you feel ready, Bear, start at the beginning, and tell your story. It's OK to start and stop. Just get it all out, a little at a time."

So Bear told the story of Bear's fall in the pit, one memory at a time. For Bear, it was an awful reliving of fear and pain, and Bear wondered if the tears would ever stop. But Bear stuck with it, and day by day, spot by spot, the black goop inside disappeared. Bear could feel the healing taking place. The tears finally stopped, and something like relief took its place.

Then one day, Bear said to the healer, "You know, I have stopped having bad dreams about falling in the pit. I can think about that time without my heart pounding. The memory has even faded a bit. I feel much better!"

The healer replied, "Congratulations! That means the black goop is pretty much gone. You have been very brave. I think your healing is complete, and it is time for you to move on."

"Hip, hip, hooray!" shouted Squirrel and Bear at the news of Bear's success.

"By the way," added the healer, "we put a good fence around the pit and installed an alarm system for protection. There is NO WAY you or anyone else will ever fall in that pit again."

Bear hugged the healer and all the staff, thanked them for their help, and left the Recovery Center with Squirrel. As they walked away from the center, they saw the sun shining through dark rain clouds, and a large rainbow appeared in the sky.

"Maybe that rainbow is a sign," said Bear to Squirrel. "A sign that better times are ahead."

"I'm sure that's so," said Squirrel, "and you deserve it!"

"Thanks," said Bear. "I couldn't have done it without you."

THE BOTTOM LINE: Do what you need to do to heal outside and in.

FOOD FOR THOUGHT QUESTIONS

1. How are you like Bear Bear? Where did you get hurt inside or out? (You might consider drawing a person and marking it in black.)
2. What do you avoid talking about because it makes you feel so bad?
3. What story do you most need to tell to get rid of your black stuff?
4. How old were you when you first *fell into the pit?*

27

Overcoming Obstacles

Some individuals are in a hurry for life to change once they enter treatment. They may not realize that they are likely to face a number of economic, vocational, educational, emotional, and environmental obstacles. When they make mistakes, they are hard on themselves and feel like "nothing has changed." They may be *haunted* by flashbacks and nightmares and fear they will "never" be free of the past. It is important to help clients persevere in the face of obstacles.

The process of change involves staying focused on goals while looking back every once in awhile to validate progress. Clients sometimes may not recognize how far they have come.

The Obstacle Course encourages readers to put some psychological distance between current and past experiences. It is important *to look back on* the past—to put things in perspective. Toward the end of his treatment, a teen drew a tall mountain with him and his foster family at the top. He had survived many abusive experiences and had done amazing therapy work, but he still feared that his abusers might return to kill him. It was a pivotal moment when he drew a strong metal jail-like cage at the mountain's base—his perpetrators locked inside, a large spider guarding the cage, ready to wrap a perpetrator up in spider silk should one try to escape. Only the police and the client held the key. During that session, he finally realized he was safe.

This story was based on this client's experience—a life with obstacles at every turn. Only when he reached the top and looked back on where he started was it clear, in perspective, how far he had come.

THE OBSTACLE COURSE

Hunter Hampster sat slumped over on a bench at Frustrate U Park, his head in his paws. "What a miserable day," he complained. "What a frustrating playground!" The sun was shining, the view was spectacular, but Hunter was so frustrated he thought he might cry.

A playground is supposed to be fun—not frustrating. But the mean man who had designed Frustrate U playground *liked* making kids cry. He smiled in a real nasty way. "Make my day," he said. "Try the swings, and don't forget the monkey bars."

The swings had rusty chains of different lengths, and the mean man had sawed halfway through some of them, so you never knew when they would break, dropping you into the mud below. While Hunter was swinging, sure enough, a chain broke and he landed in the mud. How frustrating!

Hunter headed next for the monkey bars. "I'm good at that," he thought.

Hunter moved hand by hand across the bars. When he was halfway across, he grabbed a bar that wobbled and stretched. BOING! It was made of rubber! Hunter bounced up and down so hard that he lost his grip and fell to the ground.

"F#*$!" he cried out. It was so frustrating!

Then Hunter decided to try the obstacle course. The mean man had built it a little like a miniature golf course with trees, plants, flowers, running water, and a big mountain right in the middle. If you made it to the top, you won a prize, and Hunter wanted to win a prize.

"Enter at your own risk," said the sign. Hunter entered the obstacle course but five minutes later he was still right where he started. Hunter stopped and looked around. He was inside a giant hamster wheel!

"What a waste of time and energy," said Hunter, as he jumped out of the wheel. "Good thing I figured it out sooner rather than later."

Hunter saw two paths ahead. The first path looked steep and there was a sign with an arrow pointing up. The sign said, "To the Top of the Obstacle Course." The other path headed back to the entrance, and the sign said, "Exit, Quit Now!"

"I'm not ready to quit," said Hunter, as he headed up the steeper path. Twenty minutes later, Hunter still had not made any progress.

Hunter, sweaty and dirty, frowned with frustration.

Along came a little girl.

"What are you doing?" she asked.

"Climbing to the top of the obstacle course," he said. "But I'm having some trouble."

"You're on a treadmill, you know," said the girl, pointing down to Hunter's feet.

Hunter looked down. Sure enough, he was on a large treadmill.

"No wonder I'm not going anywhere," he said.

The little girl giggled. "The mean man put the treadmill there as a distraction, to frustrate you."

Hunter frowned at her, jumped off the treadmill, and continued on.

Further up the path, Hunter suddenly found himself going round and round. He hung on tightly. It made him feel dizzy and sick.

As you might have guessed, the next obstacle was a merry-go-round.

The little girl had already reached the top of the obstacle course. She called down to Hunter, "What are you doing?"

"I'm not sure. I'm stuck on this merry-go-round, and I think I'm going to throw up."

"Get off the merry-go-round," said the little girl. "It's another distraction, to frustrate you and get you to quit."

"She's a real know-it-all," muttered Hunter under his breath as he jumped off the merry-go-round, threw up, and continued up the mountain.

Right before Hunter reached the top, there were three signs. One said, "Detour" and pointed to a new path. The second sign said, "Exit Now!" and pointed to a path going back down the mountain. The last sign said, "Continue at Your Own Risk: Summit Ahead—Beware of Falling Rocks." Hunter was almost to the top and had no intention of quitting. He was tempted to take the detour, but he had no idea where it led. So Hunter stayed on the main path to finish the obstacle course and kept a close lookout for falling rocks.

Finally Hunter reached the top. He could see the lights of the town off in the distance, far below. The houses and cars looked like tiny toys, and the people like little ants. All the obstacles were behind him.

"Wow!" exclaimed Hunter. "This is a long way from where I started!"

"Yes," said the girl, who had been waiting for him at the top. She handed Hunter his prize, a big bag of red peanut M&M's. Hunter the Hampster loved peanut M&M's!

"From the top," said Hunter, "Everything down there seems small and insignificant."

"Are you still frustrated?" asked the girl.

"No," said Hunter. "Now that I am past the obstacles, I see things from a new point of view."

Hunter said goodbye to the girl and thanked her for helping him.

Who knows why a mean grownup hated kids so much that he designed a park full of obstacles. The world is full of mean people that pick on others just for spite. But Hunter had realized something very important. The obstacles in life are not the point—the point is getting around them and staying focused on your goal.

THE BOTTOM LINE: Get beyond the obstacles!

FOOD FOR THOUGHT QUESTIONS

1. What helps you forget a little about what happened in the past?
2. What do you need to do to gain some distance between "now" and "then"?
3. List three obstacles on your life course and how you might get past them.
4. When have you felt frustrated like Hunter Hampster?

28

The Whole *Is* Greater

Becoming New and Different

The change process applies searing heat as it works its *magic*. It is a little like the process of working with glass in an art studio. The glassmaker wears protective gear—fireproof gloves for his hands and goggles for his eyes. As he slides the glass into the hot oven in his studio, it sears through the outer layers, all the way to the core. Similarly, the treatment process for trauma recovery is hot, painful, intense, and difficult to endure.

Many women seek help in the glassmaker's studio after flying for years in the middle of a hurricane—they arrive exhausted and demoralized. The center of the hurricane is safe and calm, even though a storm is raging all around. It takes great courage for a victim of relational violence to propel through the storm to the other side; and to do that successfully she may need some help and hope. The *helper* may shout out encouragement from the other side of the storm, stay by her side to guide her through the wind and rain, or perhaps even carry her at times.

Once the woman leaves the eye of the hurricane, feeling cracked and broken, we ask her to go inside a searing hot oven and change her very self, sometimes leave all that she has known. It is no wonder that so many people avoid therapy and decide to maintain the status quo!

This story describes the searing heat of the change process and the promise of the new vessel that will be formed, a vessel that is strong and complete. It is worth it to go into the oven, endure the heat, and come out re-formed. One client leaving treatment remarked, "It was not easy to do this, but I am stronger and better than ever before." Hopefully, one woman at a time, we can empower, support, and care enough to see them safely through to a more satisfying life.

THE CRACKED GLASS BOWL

The small green-colored glass bowl, cracked and chipped, rested inside a larger, blue-colored bowl. It was a perfect fit—the green bowl ready to fall apart and the blue bowl providing support.

A hurricane had hit the region two days before. It had long since passed, and the blue skies over the ocean were now filled with fluffy clouds, the shining sun reflecting down on the waters.

Whew!" the green bowl said. "I have never been in a hurricane before! It's a wonder I lived through it!"

Devastation was all around. Trees uprooted, roof shingles floating on the water, broken pieces of houses everywhere. There was scattered debris as far as the eye could see. It *was* a wonder that the glass bowl had survived the storm.

You may or may not know about the power of a hurricane. First there had been strong winds and needle-sharp rain. The green bowl had been sitting outside on a patio table, since the owner had forgotten to bring her inside to protect her from the approaching storm.

As the storm hit, she felt herself lifted off the ground. Green in the midst of black—the bowl swirled around in the storm until she somehow made it to the center, the calm eye of the storm. But the calm did not last for long. As the storm moved on in its path of destruction, she was flung again into the pounding rain and disorienting darkness, at the mercy of the storm's destruction. The last thing she remembered was being hit in the head by a flying object.

When she woke up, resting upside down, bobbing in the ocean, she was thankful to be alive. One of her friends saw her floating and pulled her to safety. The green glass bowl saw her reflection in the water and knew the storm had changed her. She had a hundred small cracks on her surface and two long cracks that went all the way through, with straw and dirt embedded in them. There were deep gouges and large chips missing on her edges.

"I will never be the same," she said sadly.

Her friend had placed her carefully inside the slightly larger blue bowl, a sturdy bowl that could keep the now-fragile green bowl safe. Without the support, she would have fallen into a hundred little pieces.

"You know," said the blue bowl, "You can't stay like this forever."

"What do you mean?" asked the green bowl.

"You can't use me for support for the rest of your life. You will need to go out on your own again."

"Ha!" said the green bowl. "I can't live on my own. I'll fall apart if I leave you. You are my only support."

"Well, there is the fire," suggested the blue bowl.

The fire of which the blue bowl spoke was a glassmaker's fire. The glassworks' master on Main Street had opened his services to all the local residents so that they could come and be healed. Many had gone and others, like the green bowl, were too afraid.

"I don't think so," said the green bowl. "I have heard about the hot, searing fire that heals. They say it hurts horribly to go through that process! There is no guarantee that it will work; and when you come out, you are different through and through."

"That's true," said blue bowl. "But the artist is very skilled and creative. They say he is patient and works *with* you as he puts you through the heat of the fire."

"I'd rather stay where I am, inside you," retorted the green glass bowl. "Many others did not survive the storm. Maybe surviving is good enough for me."

"But if you stay like this," said the blue bowl, "you will remain too fragile to have a life of your own. I think the fire would be better."

"There is too great a risk," said the green bowl. "I have heard that sometimes the glass shatters in the fire."

"Not very many glass pieces are destroyed by the fire," argued the blue bowl. "Most come out new and different. You have to weigh the risks against the benefits."

The green glass bowl soon got a little tired of having no life to call her own. Blue bowl got up every morning at 6 a.m. and the green bowl liked to sleep in. Blue bowl played poker every Friday evening with his friends. Green bowl wished she could stay home on Friday nights, get on Facebook, and watch *CSI* in her PJs. She realized that if she didn't try the fire, she would never live independent of blue bowl.

So one morning at 6 a.m. as blue bowl woke them both up, green bowl said in a grouchy voice, "OK, I'm ready. I didn't get to sleep last night until 3 a.m., and here you are getting up again at 6 a.m."

"Ready for what?" asked the blue bowl as he headed to the shower.

"I'm ready for the fire," she said. "I made an appointment—today at noon if you can take me over your lunch hour."

"No problem," said her friend, smiling. "I wondered how long it would take you to get tired of sharing my lifestyle."

That day at noon, blue bowl took green bowl for her treatment. The glassmaker had her sign consents before he did anything—it felt like she was signing her life away!

And then it was time. The glassworks expert explained the firing process. "First," he said, "I'll put you in the oven on this metal rack to soften and melt your glass. I can use these tongs to pick out the pieces of grass and dirt, to clean you up. Once your glass softens and melts, the cracks will blend together and disappear. At that point you will be malleable, which means I can put you on a long fireproof pole and shape you. You can tell me what you want to look like at the end—tall and thin, off centered, perfectly balanced, short and broad, whatever. I can add colors to the green if you want a change in your hue or I can mix swirls in with the green. I can add texture or ornamental features. Basically, you will be a new creation."

"A new creation . . ." said the green bowl. "I can hardly imagine myself as anything but a damaged bowl full of cracks. How will I know when you are finished?"

"*You* tell *me* when we are finished. Once you are satisfied with the result, I take you out of the fire and let you cool. After cooling, your glass will be smooth—no cracks, no chips, and no gouges. All that will be left is your memories of the storm."

The green bowl told the glassmaker what she wanted to look like and he suggested some colors he could add to enhance her appearance. Then the glassworks artist gently put the green bowl on the metal rack and slid her into the oven. The red-hot heat brought tears to her eyes. It was nearly unbearable, and she cried out. But then she felt her outsides and insides start to soften. It was the strangest feeling as her cracks disappeared! She relinquished control, tolerated the searing heat, and allowed the healing process to take over. She let her thoughts and feelings flow, as all that she had ever been merged into one great lump of molten glass.

At that point the glassmaker slid her back out of the oven and put her on a long pole. He began to add colors she had selected and shaped her with special tools into the form she had described. As she cooled a bit, he put her back in the fire to soften the glass once again. The searing heat did not bother her as much this time. The green bowl emptied her mind of worries, and relaxed, fully centered. She trusted the artist to reshape her and felt safe in his hands. In and out of the oven she went—it was a long, tedious process. Her very essence was being changed.

As he took her out of the oven for the last time, she caught a glimpse in the mirror and frowned. The glassmaker saw her frown and reassured, "Don't worry if you seem a bit off color at first. As you cool, the true colors will come out and you will be very beautiful."

It was true. After only a few minutes, the now cooled lavender-bluish-green bowl was a work of art, a re-creation. She had chosen a simple form, with smooth flowing lines, swirls and blends of color. She was a bold statement and perfectly balanced. One small bubble of her original green color remained unblended, a reminder of her former self.

"Thank you," she said to the artist, with tears of joy in her eyes. "I would not have believed that such change was possible."

She met her blue bowl friend outside in the waiting room.

"I was going to ask you what took you so long," he said as he stared. "But it is obvious. I am not sure I would have known you without that one small green bubble. Your essence is the same, but you are different than before."

"Yes," said his friend. "I am different—more different than I believed possible. The heat of the ovens was very painful, but the fire provided what I needed to become a new creation."

Perhaps this story will be a reminder that healing, although painful, is worth the effort. For it is not enough to survive the storm, battered and cracked. When you are ready, take a leap of faith like the green bowl and become a new creation—after all, with science and art combined, almost anything is possible.

THE BOTTOM LINE: The whole *is* greater . . .

FOOD FOR THOUGHT QUESTIONS

1. What was your hurricane (what in your life left you broken and damaged)?
2. How did you feel when you were trapped in the hurricane?
3. In what ways were you wounded by the hurricane?
4. What do you need to do to heal from your trauma?
5. If you could find a new whole, would the healing be worth the pain?

29

Mood Management

Some victims of abuse are "fighters" and find it hard to control the intensity of their anger. Individuals become angry for a variety of reasons; for example, one individual becomes very angry when he perceives a threat, even when no threat is actually present. Another individual becomes angry when she feels criticized; and quite often that person *hears* criticism in others' words. For still others, anger helps them deal with feelings of hurt or shame. And depressed individuals, with their all-or-nothing pessimism, may become angry when they feel *stupid* or *incompetent*.

Angry feelings may or may not lead to aggressive behavior, but anger can be a "hot," intense, all-or-nothing emotion. Those that experienced abuse or neglect as children may have faulty neurobiological connections between the "thinking" part of the brain that controls executive functioning (rational planning) and the emotional or sensory of the brain (Cozolino, 2006; Siegel, 1999; Siegel & Hartzell, 2003). Due to this disconnect, emotional or sensory cues indicating *danger* may trigger "fight" of "fight or flight." "I'll get you before you get me!" becomes the automatic response to perceived threat.

For someone with a *hot temper*, expressing feelings is like cooking spaghetti. It is OK to put a lid on the pot of water until it comes to a boil. But once the water is boiling and you add the noodles, you have to take off the lid and turn down the heat. It takes very little heat to keep pasta simmering, and if the heat is not turned down, boiling, white foamy water spills down over the pot onto the stove. What a mess! Feelings are like that—if they get too hot, they spill over. The following story, *Turn Down the Heat,* addresses the need to calm down and modulate affect.

TURN DOWN THE HEAT

Billy Bulldog waddled from the stove to the sink, shaking his head and snarling. He growled in a deep, menacing voice as he dumped the remains of a charred burger in the garbage disposal. Billy was very mad and very hungry, because his last five meals had burned.

Monday he tried to cook dog food stew, but after five minutes the pan started smoking and the stew was ruined. Tuesday he left scrambled eggs and bacon on the stove for two minutes while he went to the bathroom, and when he came back the burning eggs and bacon had set off the smoke alarm! Wednesday he tried to cook macaroni and cheese— but not even a bulldog wants to eat burnt mac and cheese. Thursday the dog food chili stuck to the bottom of the pan. Today was Friday, and you already know what happened to his burger—burnt to a crisp.

"Stupid stove!" growled Billy. "I just got this thing a week ago and it's all messed up. I'm going to give the store a piece of my mind."

Billy dialed the number of the store where he bought the stove.

"May I help you?" asked the person that answered.

"My f-ing stove is broken! I need a repair person right away."

"What seems to be the problem sir?"

"I bought a stove from you last week. It's burning all my food!" growled Billy.

"I'm so sorry sir. Perhaps you have a broken thermostat. Please give me your address, and someone will be there between the hours of midnight and noon to fix your stove."

Billy gave the person his address. He panted, pouted, and paced until 6 a.m., when he finally heard the doorbell ring.

Billy greeted the repairman with a snarl. The man took a step back when he saw the ugly face of a mean-looking bulldog.

"It's OK, man," said Billy. "I just look mean. I won't bite you."

Billy checked the man's identification, opened the front door, and waddled to the kitchen.

"There's the stove," said Billy with a toss of his nose. "It burns everything I cook!"

The repairman checked the stove very carefully. He checked the temperature, tried all the knobs and even looked at the oven. After about 20 minutes, he turned around.

"Sir," said the repairman, "there's nothing wrong with your stove."

Billy crouched down and growled in a loud voice, "You calling me a liar? Well, Mr. Know It All, there certainly *is* something wrong with the stove. I should know. I cooked on it five times, and five times it burned the food!"

The repairman stepped back, a little nervous at Billy's quick display of anger.

"Calm down," said the man. "Why don't you show me what you do when you use the stove?"

Billy waddled over to the stove, reached up and turned the burner dial all the way up to *high*.

"Is that what you always do?" asked the repairman.

"Yes," said Billy. "I turn on the stove and then I put the pan with the food on the burner."

"The point is," asked the man, "do you always turn the burner up to *high*?"

"Of course!" Billy sneered. "*High* means the food will cook faster and I get to eat sooner."

"No," said the man. "*High* means you will burn almost everything. I suggest you turn down the heat. The dial on your stove goes from low to high. Almost nothing cooks on high, maybe except boiling water. You adjust the temperature for what you are cooking—low, medium, or high."

"Are you kidding me?" asked Billy.

The man answered, "It's not 'one setting fits all.' There's nothing wrong with your stove, sir. Just need to turn down the heat and be a little more patient."

Billy looked a little embarrassed. "Sorry I growled at you earlier. I never had a stove before. I didn't know I had to change the heat."

"Well now you know," said the repairman. "Good-tasting food is worth the wait."

"And," he added, "may I offer some advice?"

"I guess," said Billy cautiously because he wasn't sure he wanted any advice.

The repairman suggested, "You get so bent out of shape when things don't go your way. You might think about turning down your temper a bit, too."

"Yah," said Billy. "My temper, like my stove, gets too hot sometimes."

The repairman didn't charge Billy any money except for the house call, since he didn't have to fix anything on the stove. Billy walked him to the front door, then went back into the kitchen and successfully fried some catfish for his dinner. He set the stove on medium to brown the fish and turned it down to low to finish cooking. It was amazing how well the stove worked when Billy controlled the heat.

THE BOTTOM LINE: Turn down the heat!

FOOD FOR THOUGHT QUESTIONS

1. How often do you get *too hot?*
2. On a scale from 1 to 10, how hot is your temper?
3. What do you need to do to turn down the heat?
4. Who gets you hot the most?
5. What helps you calm down when you get too hot?

30

Seeking Approval

Attachment Disruption

Women may continue to seek approval as adults from those same parent figures that ignored or rejected them as children. Their adult attachment styles (dismissive, preoccupied, or unresolved) often reflect their unmet childhood attachment needs (Main, 1996).

One 28-year-old client grew up with a depressed mother that spent most of her waking hours secluded in her room. The child took care of her mother and her two siblings, and she endured abuse at the hands of her father. One of her presenting treatment issues was her ongoing need for her mother's approval. She engaged in care-taking behaviors toward this still self-absorbed woman and her needs for approval were continually thwarted. Progress was made in treatment when she began to set more appropriate boundaries with her mother—by no longer cleaning for her and being more assertive. Acknowledging that she "could not get water out of a rock" she finally became able to establish healthier relationships that would better meet her adult needs.

Another woman had spent years thinking there was something wrong with her that her mother could not love or affirm her. Her efforts to achieve as a student and musician were never quite good enough to get her mother's attention. It was not until she had a dream in her late 30s that she realized her mother could not see or hear her needs, and the lack of nurture was due to her mother's limitations, not her own shortcomings. It was a pivotal moment for her, and this is her story.

Chapter 30

THE WINDOW

There once was a woman who loved a man with all her heart. But when she told him she was pregnant the man left—he did not want to be a father. The woman did not know how she would face life without her love. When the baby was born, the mother could not bear to look at or hold her, since the infant reminded her of the man she had loved and lost.

She said to the house staff, "It is time for me to get on with my life. I am moving to the small cottage on the other side of the grounds. Hire a Nanny to take care of the baby. She will be better off without me. Please see that she gets everything she needs."

The house staff made sure that the infant had everything she needed: someone to pick her up and cuddle her when she cried, early morning stroller walks to the park, and lullabies at bedtime. As she grew older, there were creative toys, nice clothes, friends to play with, and vacations. The girl's needs were all met, but she was now old enough at age seven to wonder why it was that her mother lived in one place and she lived in another. And she had been told to *never* go to her mother's cottage. For the girl, it was as if her mother did not exist.

The girl's sunny bedroom had two large windows showing a view of the garden and the pool; but there was also a third huge window that covered the entire back wall—it looked out on a long walkway that went from the main house to her mother's cottage.

The girl's mother walked by the huge window two times each day— first, when she left for work in the morning and then when she returned in the early evening. And sometimes when the mother walked by, the girl tried to catch her eye. Even a glance would have made the girl happy. But her mother just walked by, looking straight ahead, never glancing at the girl through the window. It was as if she was invisible. Some nights the girl cried herself to sleep, her heart full of yearning for something she had never known.

Until she turned seven, the girl had waited *quietly* for her mother to notice her. She didn't think it would be polite to yell or scream or pound on the window, but she was getting a little frustrated. She would have to try a little harder.

The next morning, as her mother approached the window, the girl stood up and waved her arms wildly. She shrieked, "Look at me! Look at me! Just for once look at me!"

Her mother did not look at her. She looked wrapped up in her own thoughts.

The girl decided to try a little harder. She took a deep breath, and, with her lungs full of air, screamed in her loudest voice, "You have ignored me my whole life—look at me, please look at me!" The girl pounded on the glass as hard as she could until the window rattled and shook.

Her mother did not look at her. She simply walked past, as if the girl was invisible.

When her mother returned from work later that day, the girl saw her mother coming and thought, "If I try my very hardest, surely my mother will notice me."

She screamed and hollered with all her might, jumped up and down, then threw a basketball at the window, but it only bounced back and hit her in the face. She pounded on the window until her knuckles were raw.

Her mother simply walked by, as if the girl was invisible.

The girl flung herself down on her bed, sobbing with a broken heart.

The door to the girl's room opened, and in came Nanny looking sad and concerned.

The kindness on Nanny's face warmed the girl's heart.

"Oh Nanny!" cried the girl as she ran into the loving arms.

Nanny had an expression on her face the girl had not noticed before. She seemed a little bit fed up, although certainly not with the girl. In some ways, the tightness of her face made her look ready for battle.

"I can't watch you do this any longer," said Nanny. "It's time for me to explain to you about your mother."

The girl said to the nanny, "Oh Nanny, I keep thinking that if I try hard enough, some day my mother will notice me."

"That's impossible," Nanny replied. "Nothing you do will make a bit of difference."

"What do you mean?" asked the girl."

Nanny took the girl's hand and they sat down together on the girl's bed.

"Well for one thing, that's not a window in your room. It's a one-way mirror."

"What is a one-way mirror?" asked the little girl.

The nanny replied, "It's like a window but you can only see in one direction. Your mother's side of the mirror looks shiny and she sees her own reflection. But on your side of the mirror you can see what or who is on the other side. You can see your mother, but she can't see you—she can only see herself."

"Why is there a one-way mirror in my bedroom?" asked the girl.

The nanny explained, "Your mother loved your father very much and when he left her, it broke her heart. After you were born, she put in the one-way mirror and moved to the cottage. She thought it was better that way, because seeing you reminded her of your father."

The nanny continued, "Your room is also soundproof, which means that your mother can't hear you."

"Do you mean that all this time, I have been living in a soundproof room with a one-way mirror?" asked the girl incredulously.

"Yes," said the nanny. "Your mother lives her own selfish life in the cottage on the other side of the grounds. If she couldn't bear to raise you herself, she should have given you a chance at a better life."

"I always knew I was missing something," said the girl, "but until now I thought it was my fault."

The nanny reached out her hand to the girl and said, "You are a wonderful little girl. It is time for you to live somewhere you can be loved the way you deserve."

The girl sighed deeply and with tears in her eyes turned away from the mirror. It was time to let go of what had never been hers in the first place. Her mother was beyond her reach—incapable of seeing her, of hearing her, or of loving her. There was nothing the girl could do to get her mother's attention or her love. If the girl wanted to find love, she needed to find it somewhere else. The girl took the nanny's hand and moved with her toward the open door.

THE BOTTOM LINE: Real love goes both ways.

FOOD FOR THOUGHT QUESTIONS

1. How are you like the little girl?
2. What advice do you have for the girl?
3. The little girl had *everything she needed*. Why was that not enough?
4. What advice do you have for the girl's mother?
5. What does the girl need to do to feel loved?

31

Cleaning Up Addictive Behaviors

Victims of domestic violence and their partners may also have problems with addictive behaviors, including compulsive gambling or spending, alcohol or drug dependence, self-mutilation, or sexual promiscuity. There are many ways that people "get high" or numb their feelings—and an altered state of consciousness can become a form of self-medication.

The neurobiological ramifications of substance abuse and other addictions are huge. These sorts of problems contribute to physical illness, increase the risk of child abuse, and carry legal ramifications. The story that follows, *Swimming in the Swamp*, is about an individual discovering a pathway to a healthier lifestyle and making the decision to change.

To start a new life, a person sometimes needs to leave behind persons, places, and things from the past. The new life can be a lonely one at first, since those from the past may not be supportive of the desired changes. Eventually, an individual finds others that support the new lifestyle and hitches him- or herself to them.

A young father, whose wife was a drug addict, took on the responsibility of raising his young daughter alone. "I finally realized," he said, "that I can decide to move on but I can't expect her to join me until if and when she is ready."

Recovery, whether from drugs or spending, takes determination and commitment, but the *clean* life that results can bring satisfaction and healing. This story helps women understand that family members (and friends) may be at different stages in the change process; and that one person may need to move forward and choose a clean lifestyle when the time is right, whether or not others follow.

SWIMMING IN THE SWAMP

Laura Labrador loved to swim, and every morning before school, she headed for the swamp. She would gallop down the dusty path and leap into the smelly, muddy water. The cattails made her sneeze, and the lily pads tangled around her feet. The water at the swamp was very stinky, because the wastewater plant dumped waste into the swamp. Waste water, by the way, is what goes down your sink and your toilet.

People who walked near the swamp held their noses and said, "Phew! What a terrible smell!"

Laura kind of liked the smell. It was almost intoxicating, probably because of all the swamp gas! Her parents had taught her to swim at the swamp when she was very young. Everyone in her family swam in the swamp and smelled like swamp water. They had never known any other life.

Laura knew that people in town talked about her and her family. "Those smelly swamp dogs," people whispered. "They get high on swamp gas! They should go live somewhere else."

After Laura took her swim each morning, she climbed out of the water, sometimes carrying a cattail she had fetched. She shook herself off, rolled around in the dirt, stood back up and jogged to school.

No one else at Laura's school swam in the swamp. When the other dogs saw her coming, they groaned. "Oh no, here comes stinky Laura!" Laura tried to not let their teasing bother her, but it hurt her feelings.

One afternoon, Laura took a different path through the woods on her way home from school. She trotted along until the path stopped at a wooden dock, and there was a clear blue lake under the dock. Laura went out on the dock—she could see to the bottom of the lake and little minnows were swimming around.

"What is this place?" she thought. "Sniff, sniff," she went, trying to smell the water. "The water doesn't smell! What kind of swamp is this?"

"Hey girl," she heard from the water. "Aren't you pretty? Where did you come from?" There was a person in a boat rowing up to the dock. The person climbed up on the dock, tied off the boat, reached into his pocket for a yellow tennis ball, and tossed the ball into the water. Without even thinking, Laura leaped from the dock into the water.

"Splash!" went Laura.

Brrr! How strange! The water was icy cold and it tasted delicious. There was no smell. No cattails. No lily pads. Just nice, fresh water.

Laura swam to the ball, grabbed it in her mouth and paddled back to shore. She shook herself, ran back out on the dock and dropped the ball at the man's feet.

"Good girl," said the man. Laura, her tail wagging in excitement, wiggled as she waited eagerly for another toss.

Toss—Splash! Toss-Splash!

Laura and her new friend played until the sun started to set; then she said goodbye and headed home to her family.

As Laura went in the front door of her house, she noticed something she had not noticed before. It was the swamp smell.

Laura's mother saw her come in the door and said, "What happened to you? You're later than usual."

Laura said, "I took a new path and went swimming."

Her mother said, "Where did you swim? You smell funny. And what happened to your fur? How did it get so clean?"

Laura told her mother, "My fur got clean in the new swimming place. I've never seen such water—it's blue, and clear, and full of little fish! It smells nice and tastes good. You should come with me, Mom. You could get clean, too."

"Laura, the swamp water is good enough for me and it was good enough for the Labradors before me. I'm warning you—stay away from that new swimming place."

Her mother yawned then and barked, "I'm going to take a nap now. Leave me alone and do your homework."

Laura's mother didn't want her daughter getting funny ideas about swimming in a new place. Laura went and did her homework, just as her mother had asked, but the idea of swimming in a new place was already in her head.

Laura knew her mother wouldn't like it, but she started swimming daily at the new place. She liked being clean and playing ball with the person who owned the rowboat. She tried to get her mother to go with her, but her mother made a lot of excuses.

"I'm too tired," she would say, or, "I like my life the way it is." Laura's mother even tried to pull her back into the life of the swamp. "Come on, Laura," she said one morning. "We never spend time together any more, and I hardly ever see you. Let's go swim in the swamp."

Laura felt guilty. "Mom's not asking too much," she thought. "And I have been spending less time with my family."

"OK, Mom," she barked. "Let's go swim together."

They raced each other down the dusty path, chasing each others' tails. When they got to the swamp, Laura's mother dove into the murky black waters, and Laura followed. The water clung to her fur and the smell made Laura gag. The swamp gas made her dizzy and it was hard to breathe.

"Isn't this fun, Laura?" asked her mother. "Isn't this better than swimming alone in the lake?"

"Mom," said Laura, as she climbed out of the swamp and shook off, "I don't like the swamp anymore. I like being clean. I guess I'd rather swim alone in the lake than swim in the swamp. I tried, but I just can't do this anymore."

Her mother replied, in a not-so-nice voice, "You're no fun. What kind of a Labrador are you? You think you're too good for the rest of us! Someday you'll be sorry!"

Laura felt very sad to hear her mother talk like that. She ran to the lake with tears in her eyes, took a swim to clean off the swamp muck, and went on to school.

Laura loved her family, but she soon realized it would be hard to live a clean life in the middle of smelly swamp dogs. She knew she might even need to find another place to live. She wished she could convince her family to swim with her in the clean water of the lake, but the swamp water was all they had ever known. And Laura had figured out that even though she could not change her family (they had the right to live the way they chose to live), she could *change herself*. She would have to let go of the rest.

THE BOTTOM LINE: Choose where you swim!

FOOD FOR THOUGHT QUESTIONS

1. How are you like Laura or her mother?
2. What is your swamp?
3. What comes up for you in this story?
4. Why would Laura's mother want to keep swimming in the swamp?
5. It will be hard for Laura to leave the swamp without her family's support. What does she need in her life to make that change?

32

Trauma Reminders

Following trauma, there are cognitive, sensory, physiological, and emotional reminders of what happened. There are things like smells, sounds, touch, and visual cues (like colors) that were present during the traumatic event. Sometimes sensory memories start to emerge in dreams or flashbacks. Physical responses to trauma memories may include rapid heartbeat, sweating, shivering, dizziness or light-headedness, spacing out, and shallow breathing or hyperventilation. Cognitive components include the story or narrative of the event. Emotional components include feelings someone had during and following the event.

When abuse is intense or chronic, or when threat is used, there is an increased likelihood of dissociation; and later there may be no cognitive narrative, that is, the person has no *conscious* memory of the experience. However, sensory and emotional components of trauma memories may be retained without cognitive awareness. An individual may react strongly to "trauma reminders," that is, cues that remind the person of the event, yet not understand why.

Family members may judge that a trauma victim is "too sensitive" or "overreacting" when they avoid situations that remind them of a traumatic event—they don't understand that a victim reacts to *cues* even when there is no real danger. War victims with PTSD, for example, may cringe and panic at the sound of a backfiring car. The traumatized brain reacts even when no danger is present.

The following story will help victims of domestic violence better understand the lingering effects of a traumatic experience.

157

THE FALSE ALARM

"Beeeeep! Beeeeep! Beeeep!" went the weather alert on the radio. "A Tornado Warning has been issued by the National Weather Service for your listening area. Please take cover. This is not a test, I repeat, there is a tornado in your area."

"Beeeeep! Beeeeep! Beeeep!" went the radio. Outside, the tornado siren blared, "ENHHHHHHHHHHHHHHHH" as if to say, "Take cover!"

A boy on his bicycle heard the tornado siren, stopped, threw the bike to the curb and quickly took cover in the nearby public library. His heart pounded and his hands grew sweaty. He saw no obvious signs of severe weather but wanted to be safe.

A month before, without warning, a large tornado had touched down on his church during Mass. It had been a rainy, windy, dark-sky type of morning. Suddenly, in the middle of Mass, the sky had turned black as night and hail pounded down on the church roof. The tornado struck, lifting off the roof and wreaking devastation. Many worshippers had been injured, and a mother and her two children had died, crushed under a pew.

"Beeeeep! Beeeeep! Beeeep!"

A mother in her home heard the radio announcement and the siren. She gathered up her children and the dog and quickly took cover in the basement. "Mommy, mommy, we're scared!" cried her terrified children, and the dog tucked his tail between his legs. "It's OK," said their mother. "I'll keep you safe!" But in her head was the picture of her church roof above her and her family being lifted away.

Some office workers heard the siren and quickly left their desks—they took cover in a large bathroom without windows. They huddled together saying, "Surely nothing bad will happen this time." But they all remembered the newspaper article reporting the tornado and the horrible photos of the destruction.

A few minutes later an announcement came over the radio, "Ladies and gentleman, I apologize for your inconvenience. There is *no tornado* in your area. It is cloudy and windy but no storms have been sighted. This has *not* been a test. This has been a *false alarm*."

"What?" cried the boy in the library. "This is the third false alarm in the last week!"

"You're kidding," said the mother. "Don't they know how scared we are after the last tornado? Day and night, we're listening for weather alerts. We don't need ANY false alarms."

A man in the office bathroom declared, "I'm going to file a complaint with the National Weather Service. False alarm tornado warnings my ass!"

And as you may expect, others all over town were saying the same thing.

The boss at the radio station where the false alarm weather alert had gone out did not look very pleased as he went into a dark room where the tornado warning expert worked. The boss's arms were crossed, and his voice was loud.

"What were you thinking of? This was your third false alarm in a week. I pride myself on sending accurate warnings. You used to do an excellent job. What has happened?"

The boss was talking to a small man with wire-rimmed glasses. The small man was the weather expert that did the tornado warnings. He was specially trained to notice signs of severe weather. His office window had a good view of the sky. He was surrounded by radar equipment to give him accurate readings on rainfall, wind speed, and air pressure. It was up to him to spot a storm, determine its intensity, figure out the time of arrival, and then warn the people.

In a timid but firm voice, the tornado warning expert replied, "Better to be safe than sorry."

"What did you say?" bellowed his boss.

With a big tear starting to creep down his cheek, the warning expert repeated, "Better to be safe than sorry."

"What do you mean?" asked the boss.

The warning expert explained, "I am well trained to pick up on signs of storms. But I missed the tornado that touched down on the church last month and didn't send out a warning. I dream about it, you know, awful dreams of dark clouds and people screaming. So many people were injured or killed, and it was my fault. I can't forgive myself, and I can't **ever** let that happen again."

He paused, looked down, swallowed, and added, "Since the tornado, I have watched the sky more carefully than I ever watched before. No more lunch or bathroom breaks for me!"

"How do you manage that?" asked his boss.

"I pee in a milk carton so I never have to leave the window or the screen," the guy replied. "And I *turned up the sensitivity* of my radar. So now if the wind picks up a little, the sky turns a little gray, and the rain starts to come down heavy, the radar goes off and I send out a warning."

"You *turned up* the radar?" questioned the boss in amazement.

"Yes," said the warning expert proudly. "Now it goes off when there is even a hint of a storm. And believe me, I don't miss a thing. I don't want anyone else to die or get hurt on my watch. It's better to be safe than sorry."

The boss got it. His employee was overwhelmed by guilt for "missing" the tornado and for people getting hurt. His employee didn't realize that it wasn't his fault—sometimes things happen that are outside anyone's control.

The boss scratched his chin and said in a kinder voice, "You are the best tornado expert we have. And there's nothing you could have done to spot that storm. The same storm touched down in five other communities that day. No one saw it coming. Sometimes things happen that are outside our control."

The boss scratched his head and said, "I insist that you do two things—turn the radar back down and take a break from the job."

The weather guy argued with his boss, but the boss stood firm.

A substitute weather watcher took over, while the tornado warning expert took some much-needed time off to calm his nerves.

There were three severe storms while the tornado warning guy took some time off; and they reminded him that a little wind and a gray sky did not mean a tornado was coming, even though his heart pounded and his hands started to shake. He finally came to accept that what had happened was not his fault. After all, sometimes things happen that are outside our control.

THE BOTTOM LINE: No more false alarms!

FOOD FOR THOUGHT QUESTIONS

1. How are you like the weatherman?
2. For the weatherman, it was tornados that triggered false alarms. What is something that triggers alarm in you?
3. How do you feel when you act on a false alarm?
4. What helps you calm down when you start to feel alarmed?

33

Regulating Affect

Some individuals with childhood history of complex trauma, abuse or neglect eventually become diagnosed with Borderline Personality Disorder. It is hard to make progress in treatment due to their *non-compliance*, frequent accusations, and intense mood outbursts. They walk out of sessions when their therapists disagree with them and have conflict in their work and intimate relationships, blaming others for their problems. Such symptoms, especially the poor mood regulation and impaired attachment, are best understood within a trauma continuum model.

Women with these characteristics often grew up in unstable, unpredictable homes with unreliable parenting. We used to call it the "I love you—slap" model of parenting. The child in such a home never knows *which mother* will respond—the "mean mom" or the "nice mom" and the child develops the perception early on that he or she is to blame for the parent's moods and lack of nurture. One such mother called the "mean" side of herself the Mega Bitch—she didn't understand that her intense moods were harmful to her children.

It is hard to attach securely to an unpredictable, self-absorbed parent, and it is nearly impossible to develop a positive sense of self while living in a volatile, chaotic environment. Treatments such as DBT, mindfulness, and ACT help women take a closer look at their relational schemas and learn to self-soothe and better self-regulate.

The story that follows is a good icebreaker for a DBT or mindfulness group. After all, it is easier to see things in others than it is to see them in yourself.

TAMING THE FERAL CAT

"YOWL, YOWL, YOWL!!" cried Freda the black cat at the top of her lungs. "Go away and never come back! I never want to see you again!" she hissed at Gaga, a small, gray cat that was crouched down on the other side of the room.

Freda was standing in the kitchen by her food dish, which was empty; and her cat bed, which was strangely wet.

"I know what you did, Gaga," growled a very angry Freda. Her fur was raised, her tail was whipping back and forth, and her ears were twitching.

Gaga Gray was trying to talk to Freda as she moved slowly toward her.

"Freda, would you calm down a minute and let me expl . . ."

Freda spit at Gaga and drew her sharp claws.

"You heard what I said!" she yowled. "You sorry, no good bitch. No more lies! I know what you're up to!"

"Just let me expl . . ."

Freda swiped at the gray cat with her clawed paw and hissed, "Yes-sssss, you want to explain. Well, not thisssss time, you two-timing pussssy. I'm never going to trust you again. I hate you!"

And as she swished her tail, Freda leaped across the room, squatted on Gaga's soft bed, and peed all over it. She shrieked, "Take that! See how you like it!" Then she raced out of the room and down the hall.

Gaga gave up. She could not reason with Freda at times like this.

You are probably wondering why Freda was so upset. Well, Freda *always* got really upset. If something small happened, Freda got *really* upset. If something big happened, Freda got *really* upset. Her anger thermostat had one setting—HIGH. Freda had been angry for so long that she couldn't even remember when it had started. Freda was a *re-covering* feral cat and came from a long line of feral cats. In case you don't know what a feral cat is, I'll tell you, because it is important to the rest of the story.

A feral cat grows up in the wild and is not tame. That is because when it was little, no one took care of it or loved it. A feral cat fights for survival and is often hungry, physically and emotionally. But it can't trust others and won't let anyone come too close. That was Freda. Her mother had also been a feral cat—Freda's mother was homeless and every time she turned around there was another litter of kittens. She was hungry all the time and too wild to take good care of her family. They didn't know what it was like to have a home.

That's how Freda grew up. But when she was two years old, a child found her on the streets looking for food, all skin and bones, felt sorry for her, and took her home.

"Look, Gaga," said the child. "I brought home a friend for you to play with."

It was soon clear that Freda did not want any friends, and she didn't know how to play. She started lots of cat fights with Gaga, who was nice enough, but how could you trust a cat that got everything handed to it? Gaga had grown up in a loving home, with kind people that petted her and gave her lots of good food. "What had Gaga ever done to deserve that nice treatment?" Freda thought bitterly.

The girl took good care of Freda, but Freda *believed* that sooner or later she would be put back out on the street. She didn't quite trust anyone to love her, not even the little girl.

"I'll get them before they get me," she thought.

The child said to her friends, "You can pet Gaga but don't go near Freda. She's had a hard life and doesn't like people." And so people left Freda alone, because they knew that a feral cat can't really be tamed.

When Freda first came, Gaga believed that if she was really nice to Freda, Freda would sooner or later come round. She thought that kindness could fix everything, even growing up in the wild. Well, Gaga found out she was wrong. Freda didn't change at all. Her thinking was all messed up and she got angry too fast. She never purred. If she was ever going to change, Freda was going to have to attend Cat-O-Lick School.

"Freda needs to learn to control her anger," thought Gaga. "It's not right for her to take it out on others. She would have a hissy-fit if other cats treated her the way she treats them."

As usual after an angry outburst, Freda calmed back down in a little while. She strolled into the bedroom where Gaga was resting, jumped on top of the bed, moved to the far corner, away from Gaga, and curled up on a pillow as she began licking her fur.

"Freda?" asked Gaga in a cautious voice. "Can I explain now?"

"Well," said Freda. "It won't do any good. But go ahead."

Gaga stated calmly, "I didn't eat your food. And I didn't pee on your bed."

"I don't believe you," said Freda. "If you didn't, then who did?"

"Freda," said Gaga, "it was the dog. You know how he hates us cats. I saw him go to your bowl and gobble down all the food. Then he went over to your bed and lifted his leg. I had nothing to do with it."

Freda thought with a twinge of remorse, "Oops—I did it again. I accused Gaga of something without checking it out." Then, without a moment's hesitation she turned off the remorse and justified her behavior. "Oh well, I can't control my anger—that's the way I am. She can take it or leave it. I'm not about to change for anyone."

Freda said, "You know how it is with us feral cats—we often jump to conclusions and get mad. But don't worry about it—I'm over it now. Sorry about that." Freda swished her long tail and closed her eyes. She didn't sound or look very sorry.

"Freda," said Gaga, "it's not OK." She said this carefully, because she wanted Freda to hear her and not get upset all over again. But she had something important to say.

Freda opened her eyes cautiously. "What do you mean, 'It's not OK?'" she asked.

"Just because you grew up as a feral cat doesn't give you the right to be so mean. It's not OK for you to take your anger out on others. You would have a hissy-fit if other cats treated you the way you treat them."

There, it was said.

Freda's first instinct was to yowl and scratch Gaga. But then she thought about what Gaga had said. After all, Gaga had never lied to her. And what Gaga said was true. Freda would never let others treat her the way she treated them.

"What do you expect me to do?" Freda asked defensively. "I can't control my anger."

"It's not 'can't,' Freda," said Gaga. "It's 'don't.' You don't control your anger but you *can* learn to control it."

Freda said, "When I feel so mad, I just HAVE TO let it out, right then."

"You could sit on it," said Gaga.

"Sit on it?" asked Freda.

"Yes," replied Gaga. "Sit on it. Wait, take some time, and don't react. Think before you spit. Let your fur go down a bit. All the things they teach in Cat-O-Lick School to help you calm down. Feelings come and go. You can learn to control your anger."

"I've never been to school," said Freda.

"Well, it's never too late to start," suggested Gaga.

To make a long story short, Freda decided to enroll in Cat-O-Lick School and take classes. Her classes were called funny things like Mindfulness, Think Before You Yowl, Anger Control, Meditation, and Stress Management. The whole program would take a couple of years to complete, but in only two weeks, Freda had learned to keep her claws to herself, and she and Gaga (who turned out to be a true friend) started to get along better. One of her homework assignments was to let the girl come a little closer to her each day.

It was Saturday morning after the second week of class. Freda and Gaga were curled up on the bed of the girl's room. "What is that funny noise?" the girl asked as she walked in.

It was Freda. She had learned to purr.

"Oh my goodness, it's YOU, Freda. You're purring!"

The girl, with a big smile on her face, slowly approached Freda. "That's a good girl," she said. Freda watched her cautiously with one lazy eye. "Take it easy," went the girl.

The girl reached out her hand very carefully and started to pet Freda. Instead of yowling and bolting off the bed, Freda let the girl continue. Freda didn't really trust the girl yet, but the gentle hand awakened something in her that had been asleep for a very long time.

By the way, it is true that you can't tame a feral cat, but if a feral cat really wants to, it can tame itself.

THE BOTTOM LINE: Tame your temper!

FOOD FOR THOUGHT QUESTIONS

1. How are you like Freda?
2. What advice would you give Freda to help her calm down?
3. What or who helps you calm down?
4. Describe a time you took your emotion out on someone else?
5. Describe a time when someone took his or her emotion out on you?

34

Speaking the Same Language

Persons with relationship problems may justify their behavior and blame others. They look outward through lenses of dependency, arrogance, entitlement, neediness, judgment, control, sadness, blame, rage, helplessness, righteousness, or mistrust and expect others to change. They do not see that others find it hard to understand and communicate with them. A significant problem in their communication is that they do not *speak the same language*. They perceive themselves to be victims of life events.

Being able to listen and communicate clearly with others requires patience and empathy. Clients must be taught to communicate so that they are more easily understood and can understand what others are saying.

The story that follows illustrates that the only person you can change is yourself. It is fine to be a square peg trying to fit in a round hole, but one can't expect those holes to take on a different shape. Sometimes, we need to sand away the square edges so that our "fit" is better with the hole.

MUMBO JUMBO

The creature from Mumbo Jumbo landed her spaceship on the runway and exited to the pavement below. There were throngs of people waving and cheering. Oh, I know you haven't heard of Mumbo Jumbo before. It is simply a faraway planet where Mumbo Jumbians reside and live in world peace.

The creature was very strange looking, with a huge head and an enormous brain. You likely do not know it, but her brain was made up of millions of crossing wires that processed information a thousand times faster than the average Earthly brain.

A man with a TV camera came up to the interesting looking creature from Mumbo Jumbo and asked, "Tell us what your trip was like? Why have you come to Earth?" The camera man knew that Mumbo Jumbians considered themselves far superior to Earthlings and was surprised by the visit.

The creature opened her mouth and said, "Mumbo Jumbo! Mumbo Jumbo!"

What that meant in Mumbo Jumbo language was, "You silly Earthling. I come to promote justice and tolerance. Join me in these efforts and we will all live in freedom and world peace."

The creature's offer was met with silence by the crowd. Unfortunately, no one understood a single word the creature said. Her brain did not function well in the Earth's atmosphere. As a result, she was unable to communicate.

The creature grew angry at the lack of response from the people. "What good are you stupid Earthlings? Open your f***ing ears and listen to me!"

She wanted the crowd to understand her—after all, she had an important message.

But the crowd shouted, "You don't make any sense! What are you saying?"

A lone person came forward. "I speak Mumbo Jumbo, but the others do not. Why are you so angry?"

The creature's large head wobbled in outrage on her long, sturdy neck. She exclaimed, "I come to bring world peace and can't even get their attention."

"Calm down," said the Earthling. "They don't understand what you are saying. You will find it hard to bring world peace if you can't speak their language."

"They need to learn Mumbo Jumbo," said the creature.

"Trust me when I say it is easier to change yourself than to expect everyone else to change," said the Earthling. "The problem is not with their ears, it is with your communication."

"How can I get them to understand me?" asked the Mumbo Jumbian.

"You have a wiring problem, so I suggest we coat your wires with a special medicine. Once your wires are coated, the signals will be smooth and clear coming in and going out. Then they will understand what you are saying.

"I hate medicine," said the creature. "It can slow processing speed or make you sleepy. In my world, we use special, all-natural herbs to treat wiring problems."

"Well," said the Earthling, "our world's medicine works the same way as your planet's herbs, and it has been carefully tested so that it won't harm your wires."

"I don't know," retorted the creature. "Why should I go through treatment to communicate with low-life Earthlings? I should just enjoy my visit on earth and then return to my home planet."

"You could do that," agreed the Earthling. "You have an important message; and sharing it will not be possible without the treatment."

The creature from Mumbo Jumbo agreed that her message was too important to ignore.

She gave serious thought to what the Earthling had said as she visited Washington, Cape Canaveral, and Disneyland over the next few days. She especially liked Space Mountain, which reminded her of her journey to Earth!

On her way back from Disneyland, the creature called the wiring engineers and scheduled her appointment for wire-coating. The day came for her treatment. It was not as bad as she thought it would be, since she reminded the scientists to stay away from her central processing unit, and she guided them each step of the way.

The day after her treatment, she shared her message of World Peace on National Television. "I come to propose a treaty between my home planet of Mumbo Jumbo and the planet Earth. The Earth is in danger of attack by planet Chip-Chop, a planet that lies just beyond Mumbo Jumbo in the solar system. The leaders of Chip-Chop plan to someday destroy the Earth. They do not believe I will be able to negotiate a treaty for peace, since Earthlings have the reputation of arguing over small, divisive issues and waging war for economic reasons. I am here to tell you that we need to focus on our common goals—peace and freedom for all."

I wish I could tell you that this one visit led to world peace. It did not. But the Earth's leadership formed an alliance with planet Mumbo Jumbo in order to oppose the tyranny of planet Chip-Chop.

Unless you are very different than the rest of us, there is probably one or more area in your life that you could change, rather than waiting for everyone else to change first. After all, when you are willing to compromise, one small change can lead to positive, and sometimes unexpected, results.

THE BOTTOM LINE: Change what you can!

FOOD FOR THOUGHT QUESTIONS

1. Has anyone ever told you that you should take medication? Why did that person think it would help you and why did you agree or disagree?
2. Describe a time you had trouble communicating with others. What got in the way?
3. Speaking the same language requires listening carefully. What are three things you could do to be a better listener?

35

Avoiding Blind Spots

Many victims of relational trauma do not "see" what is coming due to denial, avoidance, rationalization, or dissociation. Their "blind spots" prevent them from protecting themselves and those they love. Blind spots can be in one or more areas, for example, emotions, relationships, and substance abuse. Sometimes it is difficult to get clients talking about the things they avoid talking about.

A mother of four girls had entered treatment to deal with previous domestic violence, chronic substance abuse, child neglect (and the children going to foster care), having been in jail, her one daughter's sexual abuse, and the loss of her mother who had been a co-parent. She let the treatment providers know that there were certain issues that neither she nor her daughters would discuss. Early in treatment, we read the story that follows, and then the family drew a mural. Each family member drew an ostrich hole on the train tracks and wrote in it what issues she could not talk about or avoided talking about. The above issues were listed by all five family members, and that day, they began discussing those issues.

When working with women that have experienced loss, abuse, homelessness, substance abuse, and failure, the following story will allow them to begin talking about the ways in which they endanger themselves and their families by pretending nothing is wrong.

THE HIDEY HOLE

Ozzie Ostrich loved to walk and play outside, like most other ostriches his age. He really loved going across the street, climbing the small hill up to the train tracks, and then standing on the tracks. He could see for miles ahead and miles back when he stood right in the middle of the tracks on top of that small hill. He felt like king of the hill!

Now, of course, Ozzie's mother had told him over and over, "NEVER stand on the railroad tracks. They are dangerous and you could get hurt." He did not mean to disobey his mother, but it was a hard decision to make—whether to obey his mother or whether to feel like king of the hill on the railroad tracks.

Ozzie knew that trains were dangerous, but he always jumped off the tracks before the train got too close. As he stood on the tracks, he could hear the train whistle.

First, far off in the distance. "Whoo—Whoo!" The whistle got louder and louder as the train got closer. *"Whoo—Whoo!"* Ozzie felt the tracks rumbling through his tennis shoes, and the train got even closer. "WHOO—WHOO!" He knew it was time to jump when he saw the wheels turning.

One day Ozzie was walking along the tracks and saw a deep hole right in the middle of the tracks. He thought, "You know, I think my head would fit inside that hole!" So Ozzie stuck his head down inside the hole—it was a good fit. It was dark, quiet, and peaceful.

"Wow," he thought, "I like it inside the hole. It's quiet, and I can forget about my problems."

Ozzie started going to the tracks every day. Sometimes, he played king of the hill on the tracks; and when he had a bad day, he stuck his head inside the hole for some peace and quiet.

A couple of days later, Ozzie had a really bad day. He had an argument with his best friend Fred, and he got a bad grade on the spelling test. After school, Ozzie wanted to get away from it all. He ran over to the train tracks as fast as he could.

Ozzie ran up onto the tracks and stood in front of his favorite hole. Before he stuck his head in the hole, the young ostrich looked down the tracks to check for trains. Unfortunately, a train was coming. It was still far off in the distance; perhaps a couple of miles away; and it seemed to be moving slowly. Ozzie could faintly hear the whistle blowing. "Whoo—whoo!"

He thought, "I still have time to put my head in the hole, just for a minute."

So Ozzie put his head in the hole. It was dark, quiet, and cozy. He breathed a sigh of relief. He couldn't hear the train whistle from inside the hole, so Ozzie decided to pretend that the train wasn't coming.

Ozzie thought, "Can't see the train—the train's not coming! Can't hear the train—the train's not coming!" He said this over and over again. He said it so much that he started to believe it!

And when the tracks began to rumble and the train began to approach, Ozzie did not get off the tracks.

His friend Fred had come over to "make up" after the argument at school and saw Ozzie standing on the tracks. Fred saw the train getting closer and closer. Fred hollered, "Ozzie! Get off the tracks!" Of course Ozzie's head was inside the hole and he did not hear Fred hollering at him.

Fred knew he had to do something fast or Ozzie was going to get hit by the train. Fred dashed across the street and ran up to the tracks. He pulled Ozzie's head out of the hole and yanked him off the tracks right before the train zoomed past. Ozzie felt the wind blow his feathers and heard the train's "Whoo-whoooooooooo!" as it whizzed by.

Ozzie and Fred were red in the face and panting. Their hearts were pounding! Ozzie realized he had nearly been killed. He said, "Whew! That was a close call! I'm never going to do THAT again."

"Exactly what *were* you doing?" asked Fred.

Ozzie replied, "I couldn't see or hear the train, so I pretended it wasn't coming."

His friend Fred exclaimed, "That was the stupidest thing I've ever seen! You're just lucky I happened to come by!" Fred added, "You need to keep your head above ground and your eyes wide open to see what's coming!"

Ozzie thanked his friend over and over, and the two of them went to play in the park.

Later that day, Ozzie had a "guilt attack" and told his mother what he had done and what had happened. His mother grounded him to the house for a week. "I want to be able to trust you and know you're safe," she said. "I know, Mom," said Ozzie. "I'll keep my head above ground from now on!"

THE BOTTOM LINE: What you don't see *can* hurt you!

FOOD FOR THOUGHT QUESTIONS

1. When you put your head in a hole, what are you avoiding (what is your *train*)?
2. What do you do when you *put your head in a hole?*
3. Draw a train track. Put a hole on it for each family member. Inside the hole, write things that each person has trouble facing or talking about.
4. What from your past do you most need to talk about?

36

Giving Birth to
Something Remarkable

Relationship and attachment difficulties are passed down from one generation to another. Scientists now know that intrauterine stress can elevate stress hormones in the neonate; and poorly functioning neurobiological systems during the first year of life, including mirror neuron disruption, contribute to problems with attunement and parent-child attachment (Schore, 2001; Siegel, 1999; Cozolino, 2006).

What is truly amazing, however, is that with trauma-focused intervention and positive attachment relationships later in life, neurobiological changes in the limbic and hippocampal regions of the brain can be reversed. According to Bremner (2010) and his colleagues at Freud Meets Buddha, there is brain imaging evidence that mindfulness-based therapeutic intervention results in cellular regrowth and improved neurobiological connections.

It takes a concerted effort to change cross-generational patterns of abuse and disrupted attachment. One mother in treatment shared that she had never held a job, lived alone or finished school. She had married abusive men and used drugs. Now her oldest daughter had dropped out of school and without intervention would follow in her mother's footsteps. The story that follows encourages women to discuss cross-generational relational patterns, and how they might "give birth" to something remarkable in themselves in order to break the cycle of abuse within their families.

THYME TO HEAL

A large, beautiful blue spider with red specks was spinning a delicate web underneath a garden bench. As a woman approached the bench, the spider gave her a curious glance—she had never seen a woman with orange-colored lava hair, hands with magic wand tips, and heart-shaped chocolate buttons on her dress. The woman also gave a curious glance at the spider, because she had never seen a blue garden spider with red specks.

The woman sat down on the bench to rest and said, "Hello, Spider, what's up with you?" She added, "My name is Hope, what's yours?"

The spider replied, "My name is Lydia." And, then, a little sadly, "You better stay back. I'm full of red poison, and if you get too close, I might bite you. I don't *want* to bite you, but if I get the urge to bite, I will bite. And if I bite you, my poison will make you sick."

The woman said, "Why are you full of poison? Garden spiders usually aren't poisonous."

The spider replied, "You're right, they usually aren't. My mother was a beautiful, poison-free garden spider. But something went wrong after I hatched from her egg, and I became a poisonous garden spider instead of a harmless garden spider. Now no one wants to come near me, because it's not safe."

The woman stated, "No one wants to get bitten by a poisonous spider. Can't you just use some self-control?"

"Unfortunately," said the spider, "whatever filled me with poison also made me *want* to bite and hurt others. The strong urge to bite comes over me, and I bite before I even have time to think about it. After I bite, I'm very sorry, and then I swear I'll never do it again. But sooner or later, the urge comes back, and I bite someone else. I've learned to not make any promises."

"You know," she added, "pretty soon it will be time for me to lay my first spider egg. I don't want to pass the poison on to my baby. What am I to do?"

"I'm not sure what you can do," said the woman. "Let me think about it for a few days."

Several days later, the woman came walking down the path. "Spider, oh, spider . . ." called the woman.

"Here I am," said the spider, perched in a beautiful web above the path.

"Come down," said the woman. "I found the answer to your question, and I think I can help you."

"Please tell me," said the spider.

"It won't be easy," the woman replied. "I need to be sure you are ready to take the first step."

"I'm ready," said the spider. "It is Thyme to Heal, for the sake of my baby and all my children to come."

"OK," said the woman. "When it is Thyme to Heal, and a full-moon night, a spider can get rid of her poison by working with a healer. I am a healer, and I can work with you."

"What great news!" the spider replied. "Please tell me what we need to do!"

The woman continued. "First, stay away from others until you are poison-free. Oh, not totally away. Just keep outside your striking distance. That way, you won't poison anyone, especially your friends. Others need to be safe when you're around."

"That sounds good," said the spider. "I don't even trust myself, so I'll keep my distance. I can warn my friends if they come too close."

"Next," continued the woman, "On a full-moon night, right before you lay your first spider egg, if I wave my magic wand hands over your head ten times the poison will go away. You have to remain very still while I do that, to allow the magic to work. For the magic to work, you have to *believe* that you will heal. When we're done, I feed you a little Thyme, a tasty herb, to keep you poison-free. Once you are poison-free, your first baby, born from your first egg, will be poison-free. I will have to get close to you, though, so I take a risk that you might bite me before I can work the spell."

"Are you sure you want to do that?" asked the spider.

"Yes, I'm sure," said the woman. "You're worth the risk."

They said goodbye, and the spider promised to find the woman on the next full-moon night when she was ready to lay her first egg.

About a week later, the spider came back to the garden to find the woman. It was going to be a full-moon night, and the spider was ready to lay her first egg. "Yoo-Hoo!" called the spider. "Hey, lava-hair woman, it's me, your spider friend!"

The woman stepped out of the forest, her lava hair glowing bright orangish-red in the light of the rising moon. "It's time," said the spider. "If we don't do it tonight, it will be too late. I'll try hard not to bite you when you come near me, but I can't make any promises."

"OK," said the woman with the lava hair. "Perhaps the warmth of my lava hair will make you sleepy and keep you from biting me."

"I hope so," said the spider.

So the woman moved toward the spider. Just before she reached the spider, she pulled off two of her sweet chocolate buttons and threw them in the spider's mouth.

"Mmmmm!" said the spider as she chewed the sweet chocolate. And at just that moment, the woman moved closer and waved her magic-wand hands over the spider's head. She kept waving her hands until she had waved them ten times. The spider felt a quick surge of great pain while the woman waved her magic-wand hands over the spider's head, followed by a warm glow that spread through her body and mind. "I believe," she thought. "I believe that I will be healed!"

"There," said the woman. But as the woman pulled her magic-wand hands away from the spider, the spider lunged at the woman and bit down hard with her fangs on one of the woman's hands.

"Owww!" cried the woman in pain, rubbing her hand.

"Oh no!" said the spider. "I'm so sorry! I tried hard not to bite you, but I got the urge and just could not resist. Are you OK?"

"I suspected you would do that," said the woman with a gentle smile. "It is your nature to bite. But when you bit me, the poison left you. Your poison can't hurt me. My magic-wand hands protect me and keep poison from reaching my heart. And, my friend, you are poison-free!"

It was true. The red specks had disappeared—the poison was gone!

The woman said, "Now open your mouth, and I'll throw in a little Thyme. That will *keep* you poison-free!" The spider opened her mouth wide, and avoiding the sharp fangs, the woman threw in a little Thyme.

As she bid the spider farewell, the woman said, "Go to sleep, spider, and when you wake back up, you will have a new egg."

The spider fell into a deep sleep. Hours later, she awoke, refreshed. On the ground next to her was a brand new egg, her first egg and baby-to-be. What an amazing sight it was, striped with all the colors of the rainbow! It was clearly a very special egg, full of new life, and she could not wait for it to hatch.

When it was time, the egg hatched, and there was her baby garden spider, bright blue and poison-free. The spider knew that she would teach her baby many things and that they would live a poison-free life together. She named the baby Hope, after the woman with the lava hair and magic-wand hands. The spider realized she did not really know or care whether it was the woman's kindness or her own willingness to trust that had made the magic work and allowed her to heal.

We all have a little poison inside us—maybe you can find a healer to help you get rid of your poison. And once you are poison-free, do whatever you need to do to give birth to your own Hope.

THE BOTTOM LINE: Give birth to something remarkable!

FOOD FOR THOUGHT QUESTIONS

1. Is there anyone you trust as much as the spider trusted Hope?
2. Give an example of a time you struck out at someone who was trying to help you?
3. What is your Hope?
4. What poison in you came from your childhood?
5. What do you need to do to break the cycle of violence in your family?

37

Unconditional Positive Self-Regard

I once heard O'Hanlon (1992) use a metaphor of a pie to describe Self work in treatment. Victims of abuse, he suggested, hand you a pie as a gift at the first session and say, "This is me—this is who I am."

The problem is that there is at least one large piece missing. It is obvious to the therapist, who asks about the missing piece. The client says, "No, that's it. That's the whole pie. There's nothing missing."

Eventually you get to the point in treatment where the client acknowledges the missing piece. "That's not me," says the client. "I'm not like that anymore" or "That happened a long time ago—I don't need that part." The client might even say, "I'm better without that piece—the pie is more complete and healthy without that piece." The client insists that the pie looks just fine the way it is, with that piece missing. The therapist notes that the pie does not appear to be whole.

That opens the door for the therapist and client to talk about the "not me" piece of pie that was put aside on a shelf. We help the client see, hopefully, that without the missing piece, he or she cannot be whole. O'Hanlon reminded the client, "There is nothing bad or unacceptable about you. There is nothing about you that can't be part of your pie. There is nothing about you that is 'too bad' to talk about. I invite you to put that piece back in the pie." In time, many women are able to reclaim the missing piece.

The story that follows provides an excellent metaphor for dealing with the parts of ourselves we judge to be "unacceptable" (put aside).

THE UNRAVELED TAPESTRY

Donna Weaver was laying on her purple-and-green-colored comforter in her purple-and-green-colored bedroom, staring at the bright purple walls, deep in thought. Donna really liked the color purple, and whenever she wanted to get away from it all, she went into her bedroom, shut the door, and wrote in her journal or listened to music.

That day, as Donna stared at her walls and listened to music, her eyes were drawn to a woven tapestry on her wall. Donna looked closely at the tapestry.

She spoke. "I have had that thing hanging on my wall since the day I was born, and it is one of the ugliest things I have ever seen."

Donna was exaggerating a bit, since the tapestry was unusual looking, but not really ugly. It was woven with threads and materials of all types and colors. It had texture and character to it—a personality all its own, and the colors and fabrics sort of fit together. You might have heard the saying, "The whole is greater than the sum of its parts." Well, the tapestry was like that. Each separate thread was not much to look at, but together the threads made a nice whole.

Some of the tapestry threads were rough and others smooth. There was silk, rope, plastic cord, pot holder loops, strips of cloth, and even pieces of clean, white baby diapers. There were woven threads of black wire, pink yarn, and computer power supply cords. There were shiny brocade fabrics and red corduroy as well as blue denim and sheer curtains.

Donna liked the brocade and corduroy, but she hated some of the other threads and fabrics. And she didn't have much say about it. The tapestry was a self-weaving one. It was born the day Donna was born and every time something important happened to her, good or bad, another thread was woven in.

Donna had an idea. She would take out the threads she did not like—remove the ones that bothered her or reminded her of *bad* memories. The first thread Donna pulled out was one made of gauze bandage. It had been woven in when she had to get stitches in her forehead after falling on the playground. She didn't want to remember that! Then she took out the thread from the dress she wore the Christmas her parents got divorced. She also removed the shoelace from her first grade tennis shoe—Jimmy had teased her about those tennis shoes and made her cry.

So Donna unwove the tapestry, one *bad* thread at a time, until there was a pile of unwanted threads sitting on the floor of her bedroom. She hung what remained of the tapestry back on her bedroom wall and hid the *extra* threads way in the back of her bedroom closet.

Now, the tapestry looked even more unusual. There were big gaps in the threads. The wall showed through the gaps and the purple color did not go with the threads that were left. The loose threads of the tapestry slumped and stuck out away from the wall. But Donna didn't care. She had finally gotten rid of the pieces she didn't like.

A couple of days later, while Donna was daydreaming in her bedroom, she heard a knock on her door.

"Who is it?" Donna called out.

"It's me," said her roommate and best friend Jenny with a smile in her voice. "I have some of your laundry that got mixed in with mine. Can I come in?"

"Sure," said Donna.

Jenny came in carrying Donna's clothes; then she stared suddenly at Donna's wall where the tapestry was hanging. Her mouth hung open with surprise.

"What happened to your tapestry?" asked Jenny, and the smile in her voice was gone.

Donna thought, "I think she notices what I did to the tapestry." Donna decided to act real casual and innocent, as if nothing had happened.

"What's up?" asked Donna.

"Donna," replied Jenny. "What happened to your tapestry? It looks awful."

"What do you mean?" asked Donna, still trying to act innocent.

Jenny looked her straight in the eye. "Come on Donna, tell me the truth. What did you do to the tapestry? Pieces of it are missing. It isn't complete anymore."

"Oh Jenny," said Donna, "don't make such a big deal out of it. I took out the parts I didn't like and put them away. I want to forget about those parts."

Jenny replied, "It was beautiful just the way it was. The tapestry was born when you were born and it held the memories of your life. It isn't whole without the other threads, and you aren't whole without those parts of your life."

"Well, I kept the best parts, the ones that are special to me," said Donna.

Jenny answered. "Every part of it was special, just as every part of you is special. Now it has unraveled and is falling apart. It's no longer whole."

"I don't want the *bad* parts in there," argued Donna. "When I look at it on my wall, I don't want to see the *bad* memories."

"Donna," Jenny said very gently, "we all go through *good* and *bad* times. I think the threads you put away added contrast to the tapestry. The beauty of the brighter threads is more noticeable when you see them next to the dark ones. The *bad* threads add strength and help hold the tapestry together. You need to *keep the bad with the good*. At least think about it . . ."

They said goodnight, and Donna thought about what her friend had said. She stared carefully at the tapestry on her wall. She had not noticed it before, but the pretty threads that were left on the tapestry were too much alike. They were made of bright-colored, smooth materials. They had little depth and did not hold together well. They were drooping and unraveling without the darker threads to hold them in place. No two of the threads hidden in her closet were alike.

Donna had a sudden *aha*. "I am a weaver!" she realized. "I can re-weave my tapestry!"

Donna went to her closet and pulled out the pile of tangled, darker threads. She wove them back into the tapestry, using a new pattern of her own creation, so that the tapestry had a whole new look. When she finished, Donna hung the tapestry back on her wall.

Donna stared at the tapestry and thought, "The new tapestry is more beautiful than the original one. The threads are holding together better. I don't know how that happened. I used the same old threads, but I rearranged them and ended up with a truly lovely creation."

"Jenny, come see," she cried out. "I put the threads back in, and the tapestry is somehow a new and better creation."

Jenny could not believe her eyes. It was true. The dark, coarse threads contrasted with the brighter colors and the varied textures made it a thing of beauty, whole and complete. There were no more unraveling threads, and somehow everything fit together.

"You know," said Jenny, "this tapestry is more *you* than the other one. It brings out things I had not noticed before—a very nice change!"

THE BOTTOM LINE: Every thread counts!

FOOD FOR THOUGHT QUESTIONS

1. How are you like Donna?
2. What in your past would be the darkest threads in your tapestry?
3. What does it mean to say that your past made you who you are today?
4. How did your past make you stronger?

Part V

STORIES FOR MAINTENANCE

A woman in Maintenance has been engaged in her new lifestyle for at least six months and is committed to maintaining it. She understands and recognizes warning signs of intimate partner violence, including controlling behavior or imposed isolation within the community. She has a healthy regard for herself and is protective of her children. Her thinking, emotions, and behavior have gotten in sync with her values, and she is practicing what she preaches.

A woman's new way of life may include ongoing recovery meetings, community involvement, educational or spiritual activities, Yoga, regular exercise, and even volunteer work. And since most relapse behaviors occur in the first six months after making a change, the highest risk point has passed. At this point the need for therapy lessens, and the woman increases her reliance on friends that support her lifestyle changes.

In Maintenance, a woman can identify clear changes between her current and past behaviors and she is motivated to continue doing what she needs to do to remain stable.

During this stage of treatment, most therapy discussion is about relapse prevention. By now, the woman should understand her own personal cycle of violence and what sorts of persons bring out the best and worst in her. Hopefully, she has identified cross-generational patterns of risks and has insight into her attachment needs. If she has resolved past trauma, it will be important for her to find ways to leave the past behind and manage her stress on an ongoing basis.

The final stories in this book are about Maintenance—ways a woman can let go of the past and "cut the cord" to situations or persons that hold her back or lead to relapse. Learning how to have healthy relationships is a life-long process, and after only six months of change, the journey has just begun.

38

Leaving the Past Behind

Letting go of the past is hard, especially for those that obsess and worry about the past most of their waking hours. They carry around a lot of old baggage of regrets and self-blame. Some hold on tightly to "reminders" of their failures, disappointments, and perceived inadequacies.

The story that follows, *Traveling Light,* is about the process of letting go. The main character, with a little help from her under-the-sea friends, dumps some of her baggage and lightens her load.

This story is good to use within CBT, mindfulness, ACT, and interpersonal psychotherapies. Many clients carry around resentment, fear, jealousy, hurt, doubt, and sadness. They wonder how they will ever change and whether it might be too late.

There was a family in treatment that had never approached life issues they deemed too tough to talk about—yet each family member carried around great guilt and anxiety related to those life events. Only when they began to talk about past concerns could they let go and move on.

A letter writer once asked Ann Landers if it was too late to have a better life. The response was, "Are you still breathing? As long as you still breathing, it is not too late to change." She encouraged the writer to let go of past hurts and give herself permission to move on.

It is never too late.

TRAVELING LIGHT

It was a captivating sight—Octavia Octopus scooting along the ocean floor in a cloud of black ink, each of her eight arms holding a suitcase. The suitcases were all shapes, sizes, and colors. She was on her way to visit Sallie Squid who lived in the coral reef.

"Goodbye Scallop," Octavia called out. "See you later Shrimp," she cried. "Hey Charlie Clam, let's have dinner together when I get back from my trip."

Charlie Clam asked, "Octavia, why are you taking eight suitcases?"

Then Charlie realized it was none of his business and asked, "Do you need some help carrying those? Someone invited me to the clambake on the beach, but I think I might just pass on that."

Charlie didn't want to "join" anyone for dinner on the beach. In case you don't know it, a clambake is a beach dinner where people dig up clams and eat them with melted butter.

Octavia replied in answer to Charlie's first question, "Two of these suitcases have my things for the weekend. The other six suitcases are extra baggage. Thanks for offering to help."

"Why don't you leave the extra baggage behind?" asked Charlie.

"Sorry Charlie," said Octavia, "I can't do that."

"Why?" asked Charlie. "That's a lot of extra baggage to carry around. And those bags look pretty heavy."

"Well, yes, they are heavy," Octavia admitted.

"Exactly what's in them?" asked Charlie.

"I don't quite remember," replied Olivia. "I haven't unpacked them in years."

Charlie pressed, "Well if you haven't unpacked them in years, why not take a look. Why carry around what you don't need?"

Octavia dropped eight suitcases, all at the same time. "OK," she sighed. "Let's take a look."

Olivia was a collector. She collected scrapbook items, photos, hopes that never came true, feelings, good and bad memories, and relationships she never let go of. Charlie had no idea what he was in for.

As Octavia and Charlie unpacked, they found all sorts of things. There was outdated clothing, yellowing and faded. There were scrapbooks from third grade. There were two boxes of old memories.

"When I packed these away," said Octavia, "they seemed important. Now it's hard to remember why."

She opened a box of memories and peered in. "I know why I saved the happy memories," Octavia said, "but I don't know why I kept the bad ones."

"Maybe you weren't ready to let go of them," suggested Charlie.

Finally everything was unpacked.

"OK," said Charlie. "Are you ready to dump some of this stuff and repack?"

"OK, Charlie," replied Octavia. "There's no time like now to get rid of old baggage."

Together they sorted things into two piles: one was the "keep" pile and one was the "throw" pile. They repacked Octavia's suitcases with only the "keep" items. They kept stuff that made Octavia say things like, "Aw, Charlie—look at that. Isn't that sweet? Don't you remember that time?" Octavia kept a couple of her favorite photos and stuffed animals.

When they were finished repacking, Octavia had only three full suitcases: two held her weekend things and one had her special things to keep. They put the "throw items" in two large trash bags.

"From now on, I'll consider what I hold onto," commented Octavia. "Traveling light is a better idea."

Let me tell you what Charlie and Octavia did with the stuff in the trash bags. Before Octavia left for the coral reef, she and Charlie went up on the beach. The clambake was long over, but the fire on the beach burned hot with red embers. Octavia and Charlie burned every last one of the bagged items; and then they roasted marshmallows and hot dogs over the hot fire.

Charlie smiled. "You know Octavia, having eight arms is great, but three suitcases is plenty for any octopus to carry around."

THE BOTTOM LINE: Lighten your load.

FOOD FOR THOUGHT QUESTIONS

1. How are you like Octavia?
2. If you unpacked all your baggage, what are you still carrying around from the past?
3. When you unpack you need to sort through what is in the bags. What would you try to avoid looking through?
4. List three things you would like to leave behind.

39

Preventing Relapse

According to Prochaska and DiClemente (1983), it takes awhile for change to "set." Until changes are well established (at least six months), it is easy for someone to "relapse," that is, to return to former behaviors, thoughts, and attitudes. Those that live "up North" watch for signs that the ice on a lake is frozen thick and solid. If someone goes out on the ice too soon, the ice can crack. If someone ignores the cracks, he or she might even fall through. And in the spring, if someone ventures out on the ice once it has started to melt, the ice might not hold his or her weight. Relapse is a little like missing the warning signs and going out on the ice of a lake before it is frozen or when it has already started to thaw.

When people begin the change process, they are like that lake, either not yet "frozen" or starting to "melt." New behaviors and attitudes take awhile to "solidify"; and it is easy to miss signs of "relapse"—old moods return like the warm air of spring; "cracks" appear in relationships; negative habits are fueled by poor self-discipline. An individual may even start thinking that the past was "not as bad" as it really was.

The bungee cord in the next story represents the relapse process—life situations that have the power to pull someone back into old habits. Relapse prevention means paying attention to habits or behaviors that could become mind or mood altering or ones that lead to denial or avoidance of the truth. An individual that misses the warning signs may be caught off guard when the ice cracks on the lake. He or she might never realize how thin the ice is until the ice gives way and it is then far too late.

CUT THE CORD

"Boing!" went the bungee cord. Bella bounced back toward the door she had just walked through.

"Crap!" cried Bella. "I'm stuck again. Every time I try to move forward, this cord pulls me back, and I end up right where I started." She was sitting cross-legged on the floor, a big frown on her face.

Her friend Bill entered the room and sat down next to Bella. He noticed that she had a bungee cord, like a large Slinky, attached to one of her wrists—the other end of the cord was attached to the doorframe.

"What's going on, Bella?" asked Bill in a puzzled voice.

"Look!" said Bella.

First she moved in one direction, going as far as she could until the cord stretched tight. "Boing!" went the cord. Bella sprung back right to where she had started. Then she moved in another direction until the cord again stretched tight. "Boing!" went the cord as it pulled her back. Bella slid backwards across the floor on her bottom, and Bill would have laughed at the sight if Bella had not looked so annoyed.

"See, Bill," cried Bella, "it's no use. I'm stuck."

"Yes, Bella," replied Bill, "I see. The bungee cord only stretches so far and then it pulls you back."

"Exactly," Bella said. "Right back to where I started."

"Well," said Bill, "you have a few choices."

"What do you mean, Bill?" asked Bella. "I have no choices."

"Sure you do," explained Bill. "You can hunker down and stay right where you are. Or you can keep doing what you're doing—and stay frustrated. Or you can cut the cord."

It was true. The cord was tightly attached to Bella's wrist but it was not too thick to cut.

"Cut the cord?" asked Bella in a shocked voice. "Why would I want to cut it?"

"It's obvious," said Bill. "You can't go anywhere unless you cut the cord."

"But Bill," said Bella, "it's been around my wrist for a long time, and I'm used to it."

"That sounds like an excuse, Bella," said Bill. "You can cut it or not cut it. But if you don't cut it, then quit complaining."

"Maybe I'm not ready," Bella replied. "I don't feel ready. I don't feel *motivated* to cut the cord."

"That sounds like another excuse," suggested Bill. "You are as ready as you'll ever be. If you wait until you feel ready, you'll never cut the cord, because you'll never feel ready. Cut the cord, get moving, and see what happens. If you don't like where you end up, you can always move in a different direction."

Bella hung her head. "You're right, Bill. I'm making excuses. I need to cut the cord. It holds me back."

Bella's eyes brightened and she said, "I know. I can tell myself to cut the cord for my mother and make her proud of me—or for the sake of my marriage—or to regain the love of my children!"

"No, Bella," said Bill, "you can only cut the cord for yourself. That's the only way to free yourself."

She paused for a minute and then asked, "Bill, how do I cut the cord?"

"Bella," said Bill, "the scissors to cut the cord are hanging right there above your head. They have always been there, you just didn't notice them."

Bella looked a little embarrassed that she had never noticed the scissors. The solution to her problem was right before her very eyes!

She reached up over her head and grabbed the scissors. Bella cut the cord on the count of three and walked outside, free at last. She was free to go but didn't know which direction to take. "I could go North to Canada to see the moose and bears. Or I could go South to Florida to find starfish and seashells. I might like to go East to the ocean to catch crabs and watch the dolphins swim; or maybe even West to California to see Disneyland and Hollywood."

Bella did what many people do when they can't make a decision. She said, "Eenie, meenie, miney, moe! Catch a tiger by his toe. If he hollers let him go. Eenie, meenie, miney, moe!" On the last, "moe," Bella picked a direction and started walking.

Bella smiled.

"You have no idea, Bill, how good it feels to be free; even though I don't know where I'm going."

"Bella," said Bill, "you don't have to know exactly where you're going as long as you're headed in the right direction and don't go near any other bungee cords."

"The right direction?" asked Bella.

"Yes," said Bill with a smile, "any direction except back where you started!"

THE BOTTOM LINE: Cut the cord!

FOOD FOR THOUGHT QUESTIONS

1. How are you like Bella?
2. What is your bungee cord? What pulls you back into old behaviors?
3. What does it mean to say, "The right direction is any direction except back where you started"?

40

Remaining Whole

It is easy to fall back into old patterns—to deny parts of the self, to put significant problems or issues on the back burner, and to present only part of the truth to others when the whole truth is needed. It is easy to not see problems that others see and to present the image of "Just Fine." So when someone says, "How are you?' she replies, "I'm just fine," which when translated really means, "Leave me alone!" or "Don't ask any nosy questions—I don't want to see the truth." Slowly but surely she slides back into less healthy attitudes and behaviors; and she begins, once again, to justify things in her life that should be ringing every risk warning bell in town!

There are times of great stress when it is especially challenging to move forward and continue one's journey of positive growth toward wholeness. Let's see . . . Times of loss, tragedy, rejection, failure, job loss, illness, injury, or entering a new relationship that is not good for the woman but helps her avoid the rest of the stress in her life. Times like these can wear away at a woman's confidence until she starts to forget what it felt like to be healthy and strong.

So it is very important that a woman stay whole—focused and fully present, mindful of her inner stress, her feelings, and those warning bells that go off when wholeness is challenged. The story that follows is about what needs to happen when a woman starts to ignore or put aside parts of her or her life experience.

THE WHOLE PIE

The woman knocked on her friend's door and waited to be invited in. She was carrying a large pie, covered in foil. She had baked it for her friend and wanted to share it with her over coffee.

It was a very unusual pie, cut into 8 pieces—each piece different—one lemon meringue, one pumpkin, one blueberry, one strawberry, one chocolate cream, and one banana cream.

What? You only count six pieces? Well, I'll get to that in a minute.

The woman's friend opened the door and smiled broadly.

"It's been a long time since I saw you," she said. "Come on in and tell me what you have been up to."

The woman handed her friend the pie. "Here is a pie," she said. "I baked it for you."

Her friend took the pie, stepped aside, and welcomed her into the house.

"How have you been?" asked the friend.

"Just fine," said the woman, but it was not true. Her life had been a bit of a mess lately—financial struggles, problems with her kids, and a new boyfriend that kept too many secrets. But she put those *little worries* aside and tried not to think about them, especially while she was visiting an old friend.

Together they went into the kitchen and sat down to talk over two hot cups of coffee. The friend put the pie down between them on the table and lifted off the foil.

"What happened to the rest of the pie?" asked her friend. There were two very large empty spots in the pie pan—two pieces were obviously missing.

"I don't know what you mean," said the woman. "That is the whole pie. It is just fine the way it is."

"Perhaps you couldn't wait to taste it and had some before you came over," said her friend.

"No," said the woman, "that's the whole pie."

The friend asked carefully, "Well when you first baked the pie, were there any holes in the pan, empty spots between the other pieces?"

"Oh now I see what you're getting at," said the woman with a fake smile. "You're wondering about the empty spots in the pan." She explained, "I didn't like those two pieces, so I put them on a shelf high up in the pantry and left them home. I almost forgot they were there, silly me. Believe me, this is the whole pie—the only parts worth sharing, anyway."

Her friend disagreed. "The pie is not whole without those other pieces. There can't be anything in the pie that is too bad to share with me."

"It's like my life," said the woman. "You asked me how I was doing, and I said 'just fine' even though my life is a bit of a mess. There are some parts of my life not worth sharing."

"It's all worth sharing," insisted her friend. "You're not whole without those pieces. Put them back where they belong and don't be afraid to share them. After all, none of us can get through hard times alone.

Her friend had given the woman something to think about. She would go home and consider the other pieces of the pie that were hidden in the pantry. Who knows, maybe she would take them down and maybe she wouldn't. But staying in touch with her old friend would help her make that decision when she was ready—at least now she knew that she didn't have to make it alone.

THE BOTTOM LINE: Keep the whole pie.

FOOD FOR THOUGHT QUESTIONS

1. How do you see yourself like the woman in this story?
2. Draw yourself as a pie with a couple of pieces put aside. What would those pieces be?
3. What do you need to do to accept yourself fully and be whole again?
4. There is nothing too bad about yourself that you need to reject it and put it aside. Discuss what this means?

Appendix A

Mindfulness Overview and Narratives for Guided Contemplation

The practice of mindfulness in Western psychology arose from the Buddhist tradition of *awareness*, which is considered to be one of the seven factors of Buddhist enlightenment. Enlightenment is a state of being in which one is able to attend fully and openly to the reality of things, especially the present moment.

A state of mindfulness is characterized by dispassionate and sustained moment-to-moment, continuous, non-evaluative awareness of physical sensations, perceptions, affective states, thoughts, and imagery. Mindfulness is non-analytical in that one attends to but does not deliberate about ongoing mental content.

There are a number of mindfulness approaches worth mentioning. Ruth Baer (2006) edits an excellent volume that addresses the many ways in which mindfulness is used in clinical practice. Jon Kabat-Zinn developed the Mindfulness-Based Stress Reduction (MBSR) program over a ten-year period at the University of Massachusetts Medical School. The program teaches regular, disciplined practice of moment-to-moment awareness or *mindfulness*, the complete "owning" of each moment of experience. The Stress Reduction Program, founded by Dr. Jon Kabat-Zinn in 1979, is the subject of *Full Catastrophe Living* (Kabat-Zinn, 1990) and *Heal Thy Self* (Santorelli, 1999).

Jon Kabat-Zinn (1994) offers a useful definition of mindfulness: "Mindfulness means paying attention in a particular way: on purpose, in the present moment and non-judgmentally." Hence, mindfulness is the condition of being fully present. According to Kabat-Zinn, presence is experiencing complete, non-judgmental awareness, resulting in full appreciation of life. Mindfulness practitioners contend that only by fully experiencing the present moment can we accurately observe and describe what is *really* happening. Mindfulness practice also contends that if we can "hold" the moment, an "inner knowing" (higher *truth*) will emerge and guide us. Kabat-Zinn compares the mind and body to a guesthouse. Mindfulness is like rolling out the welcome mat and then welcoming in all your feelings and thoughts, as if they were guests to your house.

The approach of mindfulness may be viewed as the opposite of rejecting, questioning, avoiding, or experiencing negativity toward thoughts, feelings, imagery, sensations, actions, people, and external objects. MBSR has clinically proven beneficial for people with depression and anxiety disorders.

The practice of mindfulness results in the ability to live life effectively, *in the now*. When one is mindful, he or she is able to observe, describe, and participate in direct experience non-judgmentally while simultaneously engaging in daily life activities and relationships.

Another description of mindfulness practice is what Marsha Linehan (1993), the founder of DBT, calls Radical Acceptance. It is accepting "what is, as is," in other words, accepting whatever the universe serves up. Mindfulness practice requires a process of what Linehan calls "turning the mind" from willfulness (fighting "what is, as is") to willingness (accepting "what is, as is"). It is important to understand that acceptance does not necessarily mean that you approve, like, or find it easy to accept and embrace whatever is happening. Radical acceptance means accepting life on life's own terms regardless of your sentiment about it, and finding effective strategies to cope and eventually appreciate whatever is happening. Additionally, radical acceptance does not mean passivity, but rather accepting "what is, as is," while simultaneously doing what is effective in the moment.

Compulsion is counter to mindfulness. In compulsion, the individual tries to change "what is, as is" to "what ought to be." He or she deals with uncomfortable thoughts and feelings through control, redirection, and/or avoidance. Or the mind just "checks out" into imagination (e.g., fantasy or nostalgic memories), or other dissociative states of mind, and bypasses direct experience by ignoring it.

Another approach, Mindfulness-Based Cognitive Therapy (MBCT), adapted from Kabat-Zinn's model, for use with Major Depressive Disorder, is described by Segal, Williams, and Teasdale (2002). MBCT blends aspects of cognitive therapy with Buddhist mindfulness techniques. This treatment modality teaches clients to accept depressive thoughts and feelings without judgment. MBCT helps depressed individuals avoid getting drawn into automatic reactions to thoughts, feelings, and events. It teaches *responding* as opposed to *reacting*.

Lastly, Acceptance and Commitment Therapy (ACT; Hayes et al., 2004) is a cognitive-behavioral model of psychotherapy that uses acceptance and strategies, in addition to commitment and behavior-change strategies. The goal of ACT is to increase psychological flexibility. ACT differs from traditional Cognitive Behavioral Therapy (CBT). Rather than teaching people to better control their thoughts, feelings, sensations, memories, and other private events, ACT teaches them to notice, accept, and embrace their private events, especially previously unwanted ones. ACT helps the individual get in contact with the "self-as-context"—the "me" that is always there observing and experiencing and yet distinct from one's thoughts, feelings, sensations, and memories. Principles of ACT that are consistent with the mindfulness tradition and promote psychological flexibility are Cognitive defusion (perceiving things as they are), Acceptance, Contact with the present moment, and Observing the self.

The following section includes a set of healing narratives for meditation and guided imagery. Participants are encouraged to get comfortable and allow themselves to be in a focused state, fully in the moment. Participants are encouraged to listen without judgment, with observation of thoughts, feelings, sensations, and memories. Within a focused state, fully in the moment. Participants are encouraged to listen without judgment, with observation of thoughts, feelings, sensations, and memories., persons are more centered and aware, and within that state, change and insight are seeded and perception may be modified. Techniques such as mindfulness, guided imagery, self-hypnosis, and meditation help individuals tune out distractions and become more aware.

The narratives on the following pages may be used to supplement the material in the stories. Within the narratives are themes and suggestions to seed or cement change as women move from pre-contemplation to contemplation to preparation to action. The narratives may be used to begin or end sessions; and they are useful in group, individual, or family treatments.

PUTTING THE PAST IN PERSPECTIVE

You may sometimes feel as if the past is right on your heels as you run for all your might away from it. You are sure that any minute it will catch you and wrestle you to the ground. You may feel like you are always looking over your shoulder, waiting for the next shoe to fall, for the next bad thing to happen. It is time to quit fighting and running from the past.

So for just a minute, climb with me up a mountain and leave the pain, or abuse, or rejection, or whatever else you need to leave at the bottom, behind. The mountain is very tall. I invite you to leave anyone that hurt you way down at the bottom of the mountain. If you take them with you, you will have trouble getting to the top. For now, you might imagine that they are safely locked in a cage down there at the bottom, a cage of very sturdy material, your choice; something strong enough that no one can break through. And on the cage is a strong lock, your choice. And the key to the lock is kept safely by someone who will not give it to anyone, not even you.

Inside the cage is a guard, perhaps a giant spider in a web up in the corner of the cage, keeping watch, and ready to wrap up the "bad guys" if anyone tries to escape. Or maybe the guard is a mean skunk ready to spray them if they don't behave. And if it makes you feel any safer, you can do something to the people in the cage to keep them still—wrap them in chains or duct tape, paralyze them, or tie them to chairs. In any case, as you look down on them from high on the mountain, you will realize that they aren't going to bother you anymore. They can't touch your heart or mind from down there.

Climbing the mountain will let you put some distance between you and those that hurt you. The mountain is there, ready for us to climb. It may take awhile to get to the top. You can take anyone or anything with you that could help you. So climb now, at least to the first lookout, you know, those places with an observation deck where you can pause on your climb to watch the scenery below. Take a minute and look down. Just looking down puts distance between you and the past. Now climb up a bit further to the next lookout. If your legs tire from the effort, take a break; and as you climb, you begin to realize that you are putting more and more distance between yourself and what you left at the bottom. Rest a minute and look down on where you started.

The cage seems smaller and smaller as you climb, until you are near the top and the cage is tiny with blurry, ant-like people inside. They are like black specks inside that secure cage; and you are almost to the top of the mountain.

Take a deep breath as you go out on the last overlook and look down. You are safe. They aren't getting out of that cage and you have a great view from where you are. See how far you have come. See who climbed with you to the top—a circle of those that love, support, and protect you. See how far away the past is, now, way down below, where it can't touch you or hurt you. And when you decide it is time to go back down the mountain, you can take a new path so that you will end up in a new place. As you take a deep breath of calm relief, feel your body relax. The past is the past. Let it stay there. Wrap it up. Take a deep breath as you realize how far you have come.

SMOOTH STONES

(Offer client a smooth stone to hold. This narrative encourages participants to flow with their experience and let whatever comes up to come up.)

Do whatever you need or want to do to get comfortable. You may keep your eyes open or closed, whatever is best for you. Take a minute to let to-day's stress grow smaller. Let it shrink to the point that it is nearly outside your awareness. You can put it on hold, like putting a phone call on hold until *you* are ready to talk. Your stress can certainly wait for just a little while, until we are through and you are ready to take the call. I invite you to think about a time when you were as relaxed as you have ever been. It might have been a special place or a certain time in your life. If you want to go there, you might recall the sensations in your body and mind, sensations you only have when you are very relaxed, tuned in, and focused. You *know* what that's like. Find that place inside you where you can be as relaxed as you need to be and let go of everything else.

If distractions come, perhaps they will sound like white noise—noise you can easily tune out. Thoughts, judgments, memories, or images may wander in—take a look at them and let them move on when they or you are ready. If discomfort emerges, welcome it and invite it to join you to see what it has to offer. It does not have the power to carry you away. Once you accept what it has to offer, let it go. If other feelings or thoughts emerge, offer them a chair. They are welcome, too, only they must take a seat of their own—you need not share your comfortable seat. After all, you are the guest of honor and they are just unexpected visitors.

One summer, paddling down a river in Maine, I could see the flow of the river, gentle one minute and powerful the next. Life flows like a river, sometimes gentle and at other times not so gentle. On the river of life you take this turn or that, not knowing where the river is going. You find yourself in new or familiar places, some good and some not so good. As you travel along, floating or paddling, you may wonder whether you are moving in the right direction. When you find yourself in rough, white water, you paddle hard through the rocky depths, and sometimes it is all you can do to simply stay afloat. There may even be a waterfall or two along the way, and you struggle to not go over the edge. The rapids are OK, though, because without them you would not appreciate the calm of the waters that follow.

For just a moment now, let's travel a smooth part of life's river. As you float along and breathe deeply of clean air, you see the reflection of the sun on the smooth water. Calm, clear water.

The river of your life holds truths, memories, and feelings, like smooth stones, some visible and close to the surface of the water, and some not so visible, hidden in its depths. Through the clear water, you see clearly a number of smooth stones of many colors—silver, white, black, brown, copper, or gray, so close that you may touch them. The stones are easier to see in these calm waters—you just didn't notice them before. Stones look more beautiful when they are wet, their colors magnified, rich and intense. Even a dull, gray stone becomes an object of beauty when immersed in clear, cool water.

Feel free to reach into the cool water and pull out a stone. You feel the smooth, cool surface of the stone. In this focused state, you might notice things about the stone that you would not otherwise notice. You realize that the stone has been made smooth by the turbulent water through which it came. As you study the stone, you may pull up something from your recent or distant past. Like the stone, you have been changed by rocky times, your rough surface smoothed out. If you pull something up from the past, welcome it and offer it a chair, but not the chair in which you are sitting. Take a look at it, see and feel what it has to tell you, and let it go when it is ready to go or carry it home with you if you wish.

[Pause]

Now, orient yourself back to the room. Take just a minute to focus on whatever it is you need or want to remember and take home with you today. See it. Feel it. Know it. Know it. It's good to know that rapids are part of the river. When you find yourself in rapids this week, move on to still, calm waters when you are ready. You may notice colorful, smooth stones in the water that you did not notice before. Pull out a stone when it calls your name, and hold it. Listen to what it has to tell you about what is going on within and around you.

Now 5-4-3-2-1, awake, alert, and refreshed.

*After using this meditation, therapist may ask client what he or she "pulled up out of the water today" or whether one particular stone seemed to draw the client more than the others in the water. The choice of stones is the client's.

UNEXPECTED KINDNESS

There once was a dog named Lucky. Early in his life he was abandoned by his mother and abused by an angry junkyard manager; but eventually, he was offered the gift of unexpected kindness and found a safe loving home.

Lucky, like so many of us, had hard times and good times. During the hard times, he had trouble believing in a better life. He may have grown sad and bitter. As his life finally turned around, he may have started to believe that a new life was possible.

At one time in your life you may have been like Lucky, homeless or hurt or beaten down by someone or things in your life.

At another time, you may have been like the junkyard manager, angry and lashing out at someone you loved or at someone you did not love.

Like Lucky, you may remember one or more times when you were young and someone showed you *unexpected kindness*. When we are young, we depend so much on the kindness of others.

Unexpected kindness may be shown in a smile, a touch, words of praise, a moment of shared laughter, or compassion. As you think about it now, the memory of unexpected kindness may bring a smile to your face, maybe even a feeling of warmth and contentment.

Of course you may feel sad or bitter if you have not experienced unexpected kindness in a long time. Certainly you realize the importance of sharing kindness with others. You understand that unexpected kindness brings warmth and comfort, like a warm bath or the glowing embers of a campfire.

You might want to remember that kindness, like unkindness, is contagious, passing easily from one person to another. Kindness is worth being nurtured and shared. When you remember kindness you received or did not receive as a child, you will be better able to pass it on to those around you.

Now, take time to orient yourself back to the room. Alert, awake, and refreshed.

UNCONDITIONAL LOVE

I hope you will allow yourself to tune out distractions that pull you away—sounds, worries, to do lists, and doubts. When your mind wanders, allow it to go where it needs or wants to go; and then pull it back when something else catches your attention. As you allow your mind to focus or wander, think about what it means to experience the gift of unconditional love. With unconditional love, you are the guest of honor.

Unconditional love holds you close, like a mother holds her newborn. Unconditional love nurtures with kindness, sensitivity, and patience. It is freely given, with no strings attached, no matter what you say or do. Unconditional love may be shared in a moment, an hour, or longer, but when you feel that kind of love you know it is there. It is an eye-to-eye, heart-to-heart, hand-to-hand love; a love that feels safe and secure. Unconditional love is like a warm blanket—it wraps you up in its warmth. You can settle into it, like a child hugging a stuffed animal or a baby smiling with trust at a caring adult.

Unconditional loves heals. It makes you feel whole in body, mind, and spirit.

Perhaps one special memory of unconditional love emerges, with great clarity; a moment in time when you felt fully and totally loved, without doubt or judgment. Embrace that memory, and hold it close to your heart.

If you are not able to recall that sort of love, you may feel sadness and loss at not having something you needed so much. You may feel an emptiness that is still waiting to be filled.

Either way, as you sit here and reflect, your awareness of the need to love and be loved is crystal clear.

As you remember being loved, or loving someone else, unconditionally, you may begin to think about a beautiful garden filled with colorful blooms. You recognize the nurture that went into caring for the garden, just the right amount of water, sunlight, and tending to. Perhaps you are one of those beautiful flowers.

You see that there are no large weeds to crowd out the colorful flowers or other green plants; none are shriveled, dry, or brown. None are overwatered or underwatered. Each plant is well cared for, reaching up toward the sunshine, each one just as special as the others. They do not compete or display jealousy, as each flower and plant has its place and knows there are enough sunlight, water, and care to go around.

The image of a garden with its colorful flowers may return at one time or another in the week ahead and remind you that tender, loving care is needed for healthy growth. Perhaps you will remember to tend lovingly to yourself and those you love.

Now, return to this room, alert, awake, and refreshed.

BROKEN HEARTS

Please take time to get comfortable, and pay attention to the rhythm of your breathing and the beating of your heart. We are *all* experts on hearts—doubting hearts, loving hearts, and broken hearts. Each of us has experienced heartbreak when our trust was deeply shattered. Someone we loved may have been indifferent, cruel, or rejecting. When we are deeply hurt, we tend to put our hearts aside—we become hard-hearted to protect our feelings and keep from getting hurt.

We are not all experts at **healing** broken hearts. When a heart has been broken over and over, it is hard to put it back together. There may be pieces missing; or the edges are rough and no longer fit together.

A person's heart may be broken by a word, a glance, a harsh touch, careless indifference, the smell of alcohol, a drug high, or a forgotten promise. You may remember a time when your heart was broken by a glance, a word, or some other thoughtless action. You may not have realized then that a broken heart cries out with sadness, anger, rebellion, fear, or indifference. A heart yearns to be healed.

Hope leaks out of cracked or broken hearts, so we need to do things to let our hearts heal. Broken hearts require a special kind of glue to put them back together. You might imagine using glue made of love and patience, glue that comes in rainbow colors, like a rainbow that comes out during the rain to let us know the sun still shines. The glue is warm and waterproof. It hasn't been watered down, and it's a good, reliable thick substance that sticks well; not that thin stuff made of broken promises and unrealistic expectations. Imagine putting that kind of special glue on your broken heart—in time you might not even be able to tell that it was broken.

In the weeks ahead, carry plenty of glue around with you. You never know when you or someone you love might need it.

Now, reorient to the room, awake, alert, and refreshed.

HOME AWAY FROM HOME

With your eyes open or closed, let yourself become focused and relaxed, asleep and not asleep, tuned in to these words and tuned out to distractions. You might even want to take a deep breath to let go of any tension you carried here.

We have all heard statements about "home": "There is no place like home"; "Home is where your heart is"; "You can't go home again"; or even, "My home away from home." Perhaps you had a home away from home when you were young, or, at least, some place or someone outside your family that made you feel really at home. Wherever this was, the place or person was special. It wasn't really home, but perhaps it was the "next best thing."

A homelike place offers many things—comfort, relaxation, acceptance, fun, safety, fellowship, openness, or even an escape. Your home away from home may have been a haven, a sanctuary, a lighthouse in the middle of a storm, or an oasis in the desert.

As you remember this home away from home, you may feel some of the positive feelings the homelike place gave you—feelings of being at home and right with the world. It is good for us to have home-like places; where we may relax and feel safe. We need to feel safe and happy wherever we might be.

You may or may not picture one or more of the places or people that have been a home away from home for you. You are probably aware that no *one* person or place can be *everything* for you. You might want to reflect on what you have gained from being around others rather than on what you have lost. Friends, teachers, therapists, foster parents, relatives, and other people may have given their best to you.

Allow yourself a moment of gratitude for those that have touched your life. And now, reorient yourself to the room, awake, alert, and refreshed.

STILL LAYERS RUN DEEP

You might want to take a deep breath and let go of stress that weighs you down today. Do whatever you want or need to do to get comfortable and relax and focus. Feel free to listen to your breathing instead of my words— a slow steady rhythm that becomes automatic as you breathe in and out. Slow deep breathing allows your mind to open and notice things you didn't notice before.

Russians are known for carving and hand-painting beautiful sets of nested wooden dolls. They are usually brightly colored, the largest doll holding a complete set of smaller dolls within. Each opens up to reveal the next doll, until you finally reach the smallest doll of all.

Sometimes we forget about and neglect our inner parts, parts that fit together like nested wooden dolls. Imagine that you can open up your past memories, one doll at a time. As you open each doll, you can see clearly what lies within. When you get to the smallest doll, it reminds you that you were once an innocent, untouched child, pure and unblemished. See that child. Embrace that child. Reclaim your wholeness. Allow yourself to remember what you need to remember, and to heal.

Talk to the child within and comfort him/her. Rock the child gently in your arms and tell that child that you will protect him/her from harm. Remind the child that he/she is nested safely within and is not alone. As you rock the child, you notice feelings you had not noticed before. You realize that you have the capacity to once again be innocent, untouched, pure, and unblemished. Carry that realization with you; now, please reorient yourselves to the room, awake, alert, and refreshed.

REACHING OUT

Please do what you need to do to relax. Reflect on whatever it is you most need today. The only thing blocking you from moving forward is you. You know yourself better than anyone, and you are also the one that keeps you from knowing yourself fully. You are both the barrier and the solution. You are both the risk and the hope. You hold the questions and the answers.

Quicksand is dangerous. There are so many ways that people deal with quicksand. If you find yourself stuck in quicksand and start to sink, what will you do? If you hate to rely on others for help, you *might* keep your own head up and float until your feet are once again on solid ground. You might let yourself sink and die instead of crying for help—so you could blame someone for not rescuing you. If someone throws you a rope, you might not take it, because you think it is their fault you're in there—you think they knew about the quicksand and didn't warn you. Or maybe the person tossing you the rope is someone that fired you or once called you a liar. No way are you going to take a rope from someone you don't trust.

What kind of person are you? You might be someone that wonders if other people will even notice you are in trouble. Or you might believe with all your heart that if you cry out, surely someone will come to help. Perhaps you are someone who wishes you could get out of the quicksand quietly without telling anyone, because you don't want to admit that you weren't looking where you were going and didn't see the quicksand. Or maybe there was a posted sign that said, "Beware, Quicksand!" but you didn't believe the sign. You hate to admit you were wrong.

And what if you came upon someone else stuck in quicksand? You could be the kind of person that would lecture instead of help. You think to yourself, "Their own carelessness landed them in neck-deep trouble." You might be tempted to let them wallow in their fear and refuse to throw them a rope until the very last minute!

Or maybe you gave someone a kick or a nudge or distracted them on purpose so they would fall in the quicksand. Maybe you were mad at them or didn't like how they treated you. Perhaps you were so mad that you told them it wasn't quicksand—maybe you told them it was nice, warm, squishy mud to play in. And they went in, so it's their fault anyway. You might just let them sink and feel sweet revenge.

Whatever your situation may be, quicksand is dangerous. You know in your heart that if you see someone in quicksand, the right thing to do is to offer help, whether or not you had anything to do with them getting stuck. And if you're in quicksand, you need to cry for help at the top of your lungs and accept any help that is offered. No questions asked.

Do unto others as you want them to do unto you—it worked a long time ago, and it still works today. It's more important to be close than right. Invest in closeness over power, every chance you get.

Now orient back to the room, awake, alert, and refreshed.

WARM UP

Take your time to let go of today's stress, and think about how hard it is to get warm once you are cold. You know how it is—that bone-chilling cold that comes after sitting outside for two hours at a football game in a freezing rain, or playing in deep snow until you are wet clear through, shivering with blue lips. Your breath comes out like a cloud, and you rub your hands together to try to get your circulation going again. Everything is numb. When you step back inside after that kind of cold, your hands are like stiff, cold icicles and your feet feel like solid, frozen blocks of ice. The blast of warm air warms your cold face, and your hands and feet start to tingle. But it will take hours of warming before you feel fully warm inside, through and through.

Sometimes life is like that. It freezes us and makes us hard and cold. Some life events numb our feelings, and if we stay that way too long, we may even forget how to melt. Warm feelings become a thing of the past, and we may resort to rudeness, sarcasm, or hard-hearted cruelty. The truth is that our pain and fear froze us into this iced-over state.

Reflect on what parts of you feel most frozen and what types of tender loving care would help them thaw. You may decide to allow warm salty tears to melt your frozen heart. And your frozen body might need a warm embrace to be freed from its numbness. Do whatever it takes—stand in front of a warm fire or immerse yourself in a hot bath—warm up, a little at a time.

As you reorient to the room, remind yourself that you are not a polar bear—so you probably do not want to live in the frozen arctic. Now open your eyes, alert, awake, and refreshed.

POISON FREE

By now, you might be aware of big or small changes you are making and need to make. You might be thinking about your life differently or seeing others in a new way. You may be more aware of how your mood and behavior affects those around you. You probably understand now that bad experiences can hurt or "poison" people.

Once poison is in your system, it spreads and makes you ill. An untreated, infected wound can make your leg swell and turn red; and it's hard to walk when your leg hurts. If you don't treat the infection, you might even lose your leg. A doctor sometimes has to surgically open up a badly infected leg, treat the infection inside, then stitch it up and have you care for it until it heals. Eventually the leg heals with a nice tough scar on the outside.

The poison of abuse, neglect, or disappointment causes damage too; and someone who is poisoned takes a long time to heal. Healing takes love, hard work, and patience. Someone may not even realize how sick he or she is until it is nearly too late. Someone who is sick may forget what it feels like to be healthy.

Abuse and neglect are like that. They sicken, a little at a time. But you can heal, a little at a time. And as you heal, hope replaces the sick feelings you carried around for so long. You will feel better when the poison is gone. Go ahead—get rid of the poison, and be open to healing that comes your way.

Now reorient to the room, awake, alert, and refreshed.

FILL UP

A sinkhole under a road is not visible. It may fill up with water, and sooner or later heavy traffic weakens the road above it. Then one day the road caves in, and everyone sees the hole that was always there but not visible. The people in the car that falls into the sinkhole are shocked and surprised, but you, the road, are not surprised. You have always known about the hole beneath the road. Painful life experiences left an ugly, empty hole in you. Ugly holes in people fill up with sadness, dishonesty, anger, bitterness, or doubt.

Yes, you are the road, and you realize it is time to repair the road and fill the sinkhole so the road is once again solid and sturdy. To repair the road, first you peel off the top pavement to reveal the visible hole beneath. As you look at it, you realize it is not as bad as you feared. Once the hole is visible, it can be filled in and repaired; then it will no longer present danger to you or others.

What is it you most need to fill your emptiness? Is it love, or education, or trust, or a good job? Is it friendship, or praise, or accomplishment, or confidence? Is it forgiveness, or hope, or safety, or positive energy? Whatever you most need to fill that hole inside you, it is time to start filling it.

Imagine having a huge pile of all the things you need to fill your hole, by the side of the road. Next to the pile is a very large shovel. Go ahead—pick up the shovel and begin to fill up your emptiness. And whatever it takes, however long, fill that hole. As you fill in the hole, you may finally believe that change is possible.

Filling the hole in your road takes time, and shoveling is hard work. But you realize that when you are finally done, the road will once again be solid, sturdy, and safe. This coming week, consider what you need to fill your empty hole and start shoveling. Now, awake, alert, refreshed.

FORGIVENESS

A child says, "I'm sorry!" while perhaps offering a sweet smile or hug. Children hate to disappoint adults they love. When a child is caught doing something wrong, he or she tearfully confesses and promises not to do it again.

Then we grow up, and sometimes it is hard for us to admit our mistakes. We stubbornly hold onto excuses, reasons, and explanations for why we do things, even things that hurt others. We may be blind to how we hurt others or blame them for things that are our fault. Our actions toward others are often selfish, mean, hurtful, or unfair. Hurtful actions leave scars, and the world is full of adults wearing long sleeves to cover their scars, instead of forgiving and moving on.

Maybe we all need to be like children—quicker to say, "I'm sorry" and "I was wrong." After all, everyone makes mistakes. And we need to free ourselves of the heavy burden of self-centered "rightness." We don't want others to blame themselves for the things we did or the choices we made.

Give yourself permission to remember one or more things you did or said that hurt someone. At the time, perhaps you excused those things or pretended that they were OK. As you recall the ways you hurt others, you may feel remorse or regret, and that's OK. It's never too late to say you're sorry. Love means saying you're sorry. Then let it go.

As you go through the next week, perhaps you will find it easier to admit your mistakes and then let them go. And as you remember being a child, you will be more aware of the desire to maintain loving connections with others, more sensitive to their needs and feelings.

Now, reorient to the room, awake, alert, and refreshed.

GO FOR IT!

There are times when all you can see is the desert around you. Hot and dry, there is no oasis in sight. You get parched and thirsty, and the heat makes you lazy and tired. But if you grew up in a desert or lived your whole life in the desert, you might think that the rest of the world is a desert, too. Why would you leave one cactus-filled dry sandbox for another?

Some people say, "I was raised this way and I turned out OK. Why should I try something new?" Those people have never seen an oasis or a lush tropical rainforest; so they stay in the desert and refuse to think and feel in ways that would help them change.

If you stubbornly decide to live in the desert, you are likely to run out of food and water. The heat might kill you, but it's what you know. It might break up your family, but no one else is going to tell you how to act or live.

Maybe you're right. Maybe what you know—what is familiar—is best. But maybe once in awhile you have doubts. Maybe you will consider getting out of the desert—and creating a different life for yourself.

You can leave the desert, and move to a new place that will quench your thirst. Think about where you might go. There is gold out there somewhere.

Now reorient to the room, awake, alert, and refreshed.

TREASURE HUNT

Childhood is a time of innocence and joy at the discovery of new treasures. Even a dandelion brings delight the first time a child blows the little white wisps up into the sky. For children, even the smallest treasures are appreciated—a seashell held up to an ear, with the rushing sound of the ocean; or a colorful rock in a mountain stream. For a young child, the little prize in the Cracker Jack Box is really something!

We grow up, and forget to notice treasures in ourselves, in others, and in our lives. We lose our ability to see the world through the eyes of a child. We get too busy, and perhaps life leaves us tired, frustrated, or bitter. We may become critical of those we love and of ourselves, and we may treat our treasures like trash. We may forget about dandelions, and seashells, and colorful rocks. We may throw away diamonds in the rough, because they look black and lumpy, not recognizing their value.

Take a little time to find the uncut diamonds in your life. And don't forget to appreciate simple treasures like dandelions, seashells, rocks, and Cracker Jack treats. Remember like a child, notice like a child, and be grateful for what you find.

Now, reorient to the room, awake, alert, and refreshed.

LETTING GO

At a conference in 1994, Dr. Jeff Zeig told a story of a mother and her head-strong daughter. The mother worried a lot about her daughter. She worried about her daughter's judgment, her decisions, and her relationships. The mother could not stop herself from jumping in to help or to rescue her 19-year-old daughter, and it was wearing her out. The mother carried around a lot of guilt over how she had parented during her daughter's early years. She had not been a consistent parent, and sometimes she got too wrapped up in her own relationships and her own problems to pay enough attention to her daughter.

In the years since, she had tried so hard to make it up to her daughter. For some reason, she still felt it was her responsibility to protect her daughter from problems and keep her safe. The daughter no longer wanted this protection. She loved her mother, and she wanted her to let go so that she could have a life of her own. She wanted her mother to trust her to make her own decisions.

The mother's therapist met with them. "Go to the beach with your daughter," he advised the mother. "Take some sharp scissors with you. Tie a length of twine between you and your daughter. Daughter, you start off running. Mother, you run behind her. Daughter, if you reach a point where you are pulling ahead and your mother can't keep up, run a little faster—don't slow down, since I'm sure your mother doesn't want to hold you back. Mother, if you reach a point where you can't keep up and the twine is pulling tight, cut the cord. I think you'll know when the time is right to cut the cord. And perhaps you will be able to keep up with your daughter for awhile, so keep running until you know it is time to stop."

The mother and daughter carried out the therapist's suggestion. That week, they went to the beach and tied themselves together. It didn't take long. The daughter was young and healthy. As she ran ahead, she felt capable, strong, and free. She was tempted to slow down as the twine grew tight. She heard her mother running and panting behind her. But she kept running. The mother tried to keep up, and when she realized she could not, she cut the cord. For some reason, both were moved to tears as the cord was cut and the twine's tension was suddenly gone. The daughter ran back to her mother. They hugged, held hands as they walked side by side to their car, and returned home together. Soon after this, the daughter moved out into her own apartment, and the mother was able to let her have a life of her own. They remained close.

Like this mother and daughter, we each have someone or something we need to let go of or leave behind. It is freeing to take action—to let go of burdens when the time is right. When you finally let go, you will be able to cut the cord, move forward without the weight of worry and remorse. And if you tie a new cord that holds you or someone else back, remember to cut it when the time is right.

Now, reorient to the room, awake, alert, and refreshed.

KNOW YOUR LIMITS

The little boy brags with pride, "I'm not afraid of anything! Nothing can hurt me!" He draws on imaginary superpowers and magical thinking and fights dragons and transforming monsters. He believes he is invulnerable!

Sometimes, we grow up and pretend that we are doing OK, even when we are not. We hide our mistakes out of fear or pride. We don't ask for help, even when others could be there for us. We reweave reality and justify our actions so that we don't have to change what we are doing. We might even say, "If it was good enough for me growing up, it's good enough for my kids. I turned out OK, didn't I?" We don't want to admit that it could have been better.

We sometimes forget what it was like to be young—when you did your best and someone ignored or criticized you. We forget how awful it was to be yelled at—or cursed at—by someone much bigger and more powerful. We felt the tension in the heavy silence that followed harsh words. We forget how easily children become scared, have their hopes dashed, or get their feelings hurt.

The voice of a critical parent lasts a long time—it becomes a voice that continues to tell you how stupid you are or that you are not good enough, however hard you try. We fear that others will think badly of us if we admit our mistakes.

It's OK to know and say what you can handle and what you can't. Like an orchid, if you don't get watered or fed or cared for, you could shrivel up and die. You can't pretend a plant is healthy when the leaves are falling off and the blossoms are turning brown. So allow yourself the freedom to know your limits and ask for help when you need it. Nobody's perfect, and orchids require very special care. Now, reorient, back to the room, awake, and refreshed.

CHANGE WHAT YOU CAN

We all have times when we confuse a rock with a sponge and squeeze with all our might. After all, you can squeeze water out of a wet sponge and it is worth the effort. Once you know it's a rock you're squeezing, you can stop—there's no water in it, and all your efforts can't change that.

You have to do the same thing with relationships, jobs, and life in general. You might think, "Oh, if only he would do this I would be happy." Or, "I'd really like my job if my boss was nicer." You think you would be richer, or happier, or healthier, or better off if things or someone else changed.

So maybe it's time to accept what you can't change, instead of worrying or feeling bad all the time. Some things can't be changed—at least not by you. They're out of your control. And accepting those things, with serenity, frees you up. Just let them go—it's a little like letting go of a big bunch of helium balloons. They have a life of their own and don't need you holding on to them any longer. You may want to send them soaring, but first you have to let go of the strings that you wrapped tightly around your hand.

It takes courage to change the things you can. It's easier to not rock the boat. But don't hold yourself back. Change what you can, in spite of obstacles and fears. BE the balloon—lift off up into the sky, to places yet unknown.

Knowing the difference between what you can and can't change? That's a tough one. Beating your head against a brick wall will give you nothing but a bruised head. But don't avoid crossing a stream that's only two feet deep because you're afraid of water—the water isn't that deep and you won't drown. If you really want to get to the other side, you'll have to get in and get wet, one step at a time. So go ahead and change the things you can, and let go of the rest.

YOUR BUCKET LIST

Whatever you take with you today is a gift to yourself. You might feel better about yourself in some way. On the other hand, you might be glad it's over—maybe it seemed like a waste of time. Or maybe some of the topics got you thinking—about how you were raised and the kind of life you lead. You might even start thinking about what you want for the rest of your life.

You can go after your dreams and someday die—or not go after your dreams, and still end up in the same place. It's never too late to get an education—to travel—to fall in love—to try something new—to learn a new hobby—to awaken an old talent. It's never too late to be a loving parent—a loving partner—a caring friend—a good employee.

Someone once said, "It's not over until the fat lady sings." That person was talking about opera and how an opera often ends with a fat lady singer belting out her last song. Well it's not over until it's over—life, that is. Follow your dreams, and encourage others to follow theirs. You only have one life, so push yourself a little. Grow and change. Live life to its fullest. At least then, you'll have few regrets once it's over.

And so, with few regrets, take with you whatever will help you most to be the kind of person you want to be.

Now, reorient to the room, awake, alert, and refreshed.

Appendix B

Adult Attachment Questions

Items below are paraphrased from Dr. Mary Main's Adult Attachment Interview (AAI) with input from Dr. June Sroufe. Dr. Main developed the Adult Attachment Interview to assess adult attachment style. Dr. Main's research has shown a connection between adult attachment style and quality of childhood attachment. Adult attachment predicts some aspects of parenting and adult relationships. There is an extensive training program to learn to administer and score the AAI, and the full questionnaire may be found at the Stony Brook University website: http://www.psychology.sunysb.edu /attachment/measures/measures_index.html.

When doing a clinical interview, it is important to get a good relationship history, including some details about adult attachment. Items from the AAI may be useful in understanding how a woman views her past and current relationship with her parents.

For additional information, see the complete version of the AAI.

RELATIONSHIP WITH PARENTS AND FAMILY

Ask the woman to describe her relationship with parents and grandparents when growing up. Examples:

1. Choose 3–5 words that describe your relationship with each of your parents when you were younger than 12. Please give an example of a memory that indicates why you chose each word.
2. To which parent did you feel the closest, and why? Why do you think there wasn't the same feeling with the other parent?

COPING WITH DIFFICULT SITUATIONS

Assess how the woman coped with difficult situations such as illness, pain, fear, loss as a child and how her parents responded to her during those situations. Examples:

1. What did you do when you were upset, afraid, worried, sick, or physically hurt as a child? How did your parents respond?
2. Did you ever feel (put down, rejected, ignored) by either of your parents?

DISCIPLINE, SELF-CONTROL, AND AFFECT REGULATION

Assess what family members did when they were angry and whether discipline crossed the line to abuse. Examples:

1. Parents act in different ways when they are angry. What did your parents do when they were angry? Why do you think your parents behaved that way?
2. Do you remember any threat or harm toward you or anyone in your family? Please describe (hitting and leaving marks, pushing or shoving, name calling, throwing, burning, locking in closets, choking, pulling gun or weapon, threatening abandonment or harm).

ADULT RELATIONSHIP WITH PARENTS
AND IMPACT OF CHILDHOOD

Assess current relationship with parents and perceived connection between childhood and adulthood. Examples:

1. What is your relationship like now with your parents (or remaining parent)? Have there been changes in your relationship?
2. How do you think your relationship with your parents affected how you are as an adult?

References

Ainsworth, M., et al. 1978. *Patterns of attachment: A psychological study of the strange situation.* Hillsdale, NJ: Erlbaum.

Baer, R. A., ed. 2006. *Mindfulness-based treatment approaches: Clinician's guide to evidence base and applications (practical resources for the mental health professional).* Burlington, MA: Academic Press (Elsevier).

Bowlby, J. 1988. *A secure base: Clinical applications of attachment theory.* London: Routledge.

Bremner, J. D. 2002. *Does stress damage the brain?* New York: Norton.

———. 2010. *Neuroscience and brain imaging of trauma-related mental disorders.* Freud Meets Buddha, Chicago, March.

———. 2010. *Trauma and neuroscience: The connection.* Freud Meets Buddha, Chicago, March.

Briere, J. 2010. *Integrating mindfulness into trauma therapy.* Freud Meets Buddha, Chicago, March.

———. 2010. *Reconsidering trauma: Treatment advances, relational issues and mindfulness.* Freud Meets Buddha, Chicago, March.

———. 2010. *Understanding and treating complex psychological trauma.* Freud Meets Buddha, Chicago, March.

Briere, J., and C. E. Jordan. 2009. The relationship between childhood maltreatment, moderating variables, and adult psychological difficulties in women: An overview. *Trauma, Violence, and Abuse: A Review Journal* 10, 375–88.

Briere, J., and C. Langtree. 2008. *Integrative treatment of complex trauma for adolescents (ITCA): A guide for the treatment of multiply-traumatized youth.* National Child Traumatic Stress Network: MCAVIC-USC.

Burns, G. 2007. *Healing with stories: Your casebook collection for using therapeutic metaphors.* New York: Wiley.

Cohen, J., A. Mannarino, and E. Deblinger. 2006. *Treating trauma and traumatic grief in children and adolescents.* New York: Guilford.

Cicchetti, D., and D. Barnett. 1991. Attachment organization in maltreated pre-schoolers. *Development and Psychopathology* 3, 397–411.

Cozolino, L. 2006. *The neuroscience of human relationships: Attachment and the developing social brain* (Norton Series on Interpersonal Neurobiology). New York: Norton.

Cummings, E. M., P. T. Davies, and S. B. Campbell. 2000. *Developmental psychopathology and family process: Theory, research, and clinical implications.* New York: Guilford.

DiClemente, C., and M. Valasquez. 2002. Motivational interviewing and the stages of change. In W. R. Miller & S. Rolinick, eds., *Motivational interviewing: Preparing people for change,* 2nd ed. New York: Guilford.

Dozier, M., K. C. Stovall, K. E. Albus, and B. Bates. 2001. Attachment for infants in foster care: The role of caregiver state of mind. *Child Development* 72, 1467–77.

Hayes, S., V. Follette, and M. Linehan. 2004. *Mindfulness and acceptance: Expanding the cognitive-behavioral tradition.* New York: Guilford.

Hayes, S., and K. Strosahl. 2010. *A practical guide to acceptance and commitment therapy.* New York: Springer.

Intimate Partner Violence (IPV) Fact Sheet. n.d. http://www.cdc.gov/ncipc/dvp/ipv (accessed March 6, 2011).

Kabat-Zinn, J. 1990. *Full catastrophe living: Using the wisdom of your body and mind to face stress, pain, and illness.* New York: Bantam Dell.

———. 1994. *Wherever you go, there you are: Mindfulness meditation in everyday life.* New York: Hyperion.

Kinniburgh, K., M. Blaustein, J. Spinnazzola, and B. Van der Kolk. 2005. Attachment, self-regulation & competency. *Psychiatric Annals,* 424–30.

Linehan, M. 1993. *Cognitive-behavioral treatment of borderline personality disorder.* New York: Guilford.

Main, M. 1996. Introduction to the special section on attachment and psychopathology: Overview of the field of attachment. *Journal of Consulting and Clinical Psychology* 64, no. 2 (April), 237–43.

———. 2000. The adult attachment interview: Fear, attention, safety and discourse processes. *Journal of the American Psychoanalytic Association* 48, 1055–96.

McCollum, D. 2006. Child maltreatment and brain development. *Minnesota Medicine* 89, no. 3 (March), 48–50.

Murphy, C., and R. Maiuro, eds. 2009. *Motivational interviewing and stages of change in intimate partner violence.* New York: Springer.

O'Hanlon, B. 1992. *Solution-oriented hypnosis for inner healing.* Workshop. Nashville, TN: Solutions, Inc.

Perry, B., and M. Szalavitz. 2006. *The boy who was raised as a dog: And other stories from a child psychiatrist's notebook—What traumatized children can teach us about loss, love and healing.* New York: Basic Books.

Praissman, S. 2008. Mindfulness-based stress reduction: A literature review and clinician's guide. *Journal of the Academy of Nurse Practitioners* 20, no. 4, 212–16.

Prochaska, J., and C. DiClemente. 1983. Stages and processes of self-change of smoking: Toward an integrative model of change. *Journal of Consulting and Clinical Psychology* 51, 390–95.

Prochaska, J. O., and W. F. Velicer. 1997. The transtheoretical model of health behavior change. *American Journal of Health Promotion* 12, 38–48.

Rathus, J., N. Cavuoto, and V. Passarelli. 2006. Dialectical behavior therapy (dbt): A mindfulness-based treatment for intimate partner violence. In R. A. Baer, ed., *Mindfulness-Based Treatment Approaches: Clinician's Guide to Evidence Base and Applications (Practical Resources for the Mental Health Professional)*. Burlington, MA: Academic Press (Elsevier).

Ross, Colin. 2010. *The dissociative structural model: A way of understanding PTSD.* Freud Meets Buddha, Chicago, March.

——. 2010. *Trauma model therapy: Principles and strategies.* Freud Meets Buddha, Chicago, March.

Santorelli, S. 1999. *Heal thy self: Lessons on mindfulness in medicine.* New York: Crown Publishers.

Schore, A. 2001. The effects of a secure attachment relationship on right brain development, affect regulation, and infant mental health. *Infant Mental Health Journal* 22, 7–66.

Segal, Z., J. Williams, and J. Teasdale. 2002. *Mindfulness-based cognitive therapy for depression: A new approach to preventing relapse.* New York: Guilford.

Sfroufe, L., A. Carlson, K. Levy, and B. Egeland. 1999. Implications of attachment theory for developmental psychopathology. *Development and Psychopathology* 11, 1–13.

Siegel, D. J. 1999. *The developing mind.* New York: Guilford.

Siegel, D. J., and M. Hartzell. 2003. *Parenting from the inside out: How a deeper self-understanding can help you raise children who thrive.* New York: Penguin.

Singer, J. B. 2009. Prochaska and DiClemente's Stages of Change Model for Social Workers (Episode 53). *Social Work Podcast.* http://socialworkpodcast .com/2009/10/prochaska-and-diclementes-stages-of.html. October 10.

Summit for Clinical Excellence. 2010. Freud meets Buddha: Mindfulness as a therapeutic tool for healing trauma. Chicago, March 18–20.

Thompson, R. A. 1999. Early attachment and later development. In J. Cassidy and P. R. Shaver, eds., *Handbook of Attachment: Theory, Research, and Clinical Applications.* New York: Guilford.

Zeanah, C. H., J. A. Larrieu, S. S. Heller, and J. Valliere. 2000. Infant-parent relationship assessment. In C. Zeanah, ed., *Handbook of Infant Mental Health*, 2nd ed., 222–35. New York: Guilford.

Zeig, J. 2008. *The utilization of Ericksonian method in couples and family therapy.* Workshop. Louisville, KY.

Index

About the Author

Pat Pernicano, licensed psychologist, has been director of clinical services at Providence House for Children since 2007, as well as associate clinical faculty at Spalding University since 1996. Pernicano develops, implements, and supervises treatment interventions for trauma resolution in children, adults, and families. She is the author of *Metaphorical Stories for Child Therapy: Of Magic and Miracles* and *Family-Focused Trauma Intervention: Using Metaphor and Play with Victims of Abuse and Neglect* (both Jason Aronson, 2010).

Pernicano has a growing interest in the Transtheoretical Stages of Change Model as it applies to domestic violence recovery and has clinical and teaching interests in applied developmental psychology, personality assessment, child and family therapy, trauma-focused CBT, PTSD/complex trauma, neurobiology of trauma, and play therapies. She has presented workshops on *The Use of Metaphor and Play in Implementing TF-CBT* and on *Metaphor and Play in Family-Focused Treatment*.

Pernicano resides in Louisville, Kentucky, and enjoys RV travel with her psychologist husband, Kevin, whenever possible.